WHO IS MY LIEGE?

By the same author

WHO IS MY LIEGE?

A Study of Loyalty and Betrayal in our Time

George K. Young

GENTRY BOOKS · LONDON

© G. K. Young 1972
First published 1972
SBN 85614 008 2

Published by GENTRY BOOKS LIMITED
55–61 Moorgate, London, EC2R 6BR
Designed by Brian Roll
Printed by THE ANCHOR PRESS LIMITED
Tiptree, Essex

Acknowledgements

The author wishes to thank the authors and publishers of the following works for permission to reprint copyright material: *Prospect for Metaphysics* by Ian T. Ramsey, George Allen & Unwin Ltd; *Man on His Nature* by Sir Charles Sherrington, Cambridge University Press; *The Charm of Politics* by R. H. S. Crossman, Hamish Hamilton Ltd; *Israel: The Sword and the Harp* by Ferdynand Zweig, Heinemann Educational Books Ltd; *An Essay on Liberation* by Herbert Marcuse, and *Student Casualties* by Anthony Ryle, Penguin Books Ltd; *Feudal Society* by Marc Bloch, Routledge & Kegan Paul Ltd.

Contents

I. Deceive
and Rule

I. Deceive and Rule

Can a society survive without a common loyalty? Or can a substitute be found—one of function, of interest, or of communication—to take the place of 'faithful adherence', to use the dictionary definition? One hundred years ago there might have been argument as to the objects of loyalty but the questions themselves would have been irrelevant. Fifty years ago the questions had become relevant—at least for Russians, Germans, and Austrians. To-day, apart from Switzerland, it is hardly possible to identify an unquestioned loyalty to any contemporary state while formal allegiances throughout the Western world appear to be undergoing something more than the stresses and interpretations to which they are normally subject from social and political change.

In Britain the underlying unease over what can overtake a society without the safeguard of a corporate sense of loyalty has now broken surface. It was our licensed stirrer-up of political hornets' nests, Mr. Enoch Powell, who first advocated the need for closer control of 'substantial elements which do not identify themselves with the rest of the institution or community or nation'.[1] Powell, usually right in principle although sometimes wrong in substance, was not strictly correct about the elements he then had in mind, namely the Southern Irish, whose identification with the English, whatever strange forms it may take, is for better or worse complete as it swings wildly from hate to love and back again: without the English the Irish could not exist. But the British Left's outburst of fury indicated that once again Powell had touched some raw nerve in the body politick and uncovered uncertainty in the Left's faith in its own dogma. A year later he roused their fury even more when he asked—not without justification—whether deliberate manipulations and suppressions of truth and fact over Britain's future did not reflect infiltration of enemies of the country into departments of State.[2]

[1] Speech to Wolverhampton Constituency Association, 28.8.69.
[2] Speech to Wolverhampton Constituency Association, 11.6.70.

But only a month after this without any *amende honorable, The Times* newspaper, which had led the chorus of denunciation against Powell, had to admit: 'At the moment it is the freedom not of minorities but of the majority that is under attack—the freedom of ordinary citizens not to have their own and their children's environment conditioned by people with an interest in the destruction of a culture.'[3] And by the autumn the British Prime Minister told the United Nations General Assembly: 'We must recognize a new threat to the peace of the nations, indeed to the fabric of society. We have seen in the last few years the growth of a cult of political violence, preached and practised not so much between states as within them. It may be that in the 1970's civil war will be the main danger we will face.'[4] The decision to expel the German student, Rudi Dutschke, certainly indicated a new sensitivity—thought by some to be an over-sensitivity—to threats to national security and in the same month of January 1971, as if to underline a new element at work in the British political scene, off went bombs round the residence of a Cabinet Minister.

If a new form of treason is abroad, it is matched by the concept of loyalty being stretched to disbelief. The university debating motions of the thirties on whether or not to fight for King and Country look strangely dated when there is even constitutional doubt as to what constitutes a British nation. Is a liege bound to render allegiance and service? For there is no reconciliation in logic between Miss Bernadette Devlin's oath of allegiance on taking her Parliamentary seat and her non-Parliamentary conduct, nor between the automatic acceptance as 'citizens of the United Kingdom' of immigrants from Commonwealth territories which have deliberately rejected allegiance to the Crown. The Monarchy itself responds to loyalty—as with the Rhodesians—by declaring it rebellion in order to serve the expediencies of Labour policy. A member of the House of Commons—appropriately enough a Mr. Michael English—tabled a motion in July 1970 that newly elected M.P.s need no longer swear or affirm allegiance to the Crown. At least this was pushing the issue of formal loyalty to its logical conclusion. None is required!

In no age has all been loyalty and light. The instigators of betrayal were generally the liege lords rather than their men. And when faith in a cause was its only strength, treachery has often been at its blackest.

[3] 23.7.70.
[4] 23.9.70.

The abandonment of Montrose who had put all to the test for the sake of the 'great, good, and just' was only partly atoned by Charles's own execution: the dynasty never recovered credit among the totality of its subjects although the Stuarts were no worse than their predecessors. Probing further back among mediæval illuminations and manuscripts, it requires an effort to visualize the treachery and cruelty associated with the gothic gestures, outsize diadems and orbs, and stiff robes of emperors and prelates. In the even stiffer Latin or Middle High German of the texts their statecraft and cunning acquire the conventional acceptability of stained-glass adornment so that only the outward magnificence remains.

Yet contemporary chroniclers return again and again to the underlying incongruity. The feudal order, as its name indicates, was ostensibly founded on trust and loyalty, on the vassal placing his hands between those of his lord and swearing fealty, and on the lord accepting the mutual obligations by a formal exchange of kisses. The records on the other hand are an unremitting tale of pledges broken, safe-conducts revoked, conspiracies in peace and treachery in war, and contemporaries recognized betrayal for what it was. 'O thou German land', sighed the minnesinger Walter von der Vogelweide at the miseries suffered by the people from the intrigues of popes and emperors over issues of power and rule. The mystery is that from this tangled skein of betrayal by rulers and of savage revolt by betrayed subjects emerged Europe's most passionate loyalty, that of nationalism.

So what loyalty will emerge from contemporary treachery? Patriotism may on occasion have been the scoundrel's refuge but whether in power or in protest the alternative of Marxism hardly produces paragons of solidarity. And in the Western world there is an all-pervading smell of betrayal as characteristic as the unmistakable mixture of urine and oil fumes which hits the nostrils of the traveller to the Middle East or the peculiar *bouquet d'Afrique* which persists from Sahara to Zambesi. The concentration of odour is not around the obvious cases, such as my erstwhile colleagues, George Blake and Kim Philby. It seems to settle round politicians, senior civil servants, members of high tables and boardrooms—those tall amiable Englishmen on whose lips one so often hears the phrase 'Honour demands . . .' when their role at home and overseas has been abandonment of some community or individual, black, brown, or white, who had relied on their word. Forming the rearguard of withdrawal from Empire doubtless involved petty deceits. But at home too there has been a growing sense of being let down. Were the so-called traitors only paying us back in our own coin?

This is no sudden development. Coming to political consciousness in a Liberal household of the post-World War One world, I was early made aware that some major sell-out was in progress. Who were these treacherous scallywags against whom grandfathers were fuming? It was something of a surprise to see their pictures in the papers—very dignified gentlemen in frock coats leaving Westminster Abbey or St. Margaret's Westminster after some memorial service. They seem to have been burying a lot of Liberals in those days! Since one's grandfather could not be wrong, the basis of political scepticism was laid. And when one now reads the letters and diaries of the years 1919–1923 and of the agreement on one side by Lloyd George and his Chief Whip, F. E. Guest, and on the other by the Tory leadership to secure votes for Conservatives against Liberal parliamentary candidates, it is hard to conceive how political betrayal could go further. Among the Liberals Sir Donald Maclean—father of the notorious spy—and among the Tories Bonar Law emerge as the only two upright men of the last days of the Liberal–Conservative Coalition. Liberalism still remained a mass faith for another decade and there were still those who believed in the Welsh wizard, but others chanted not without reason:

> Lloyd George no doubt
> When his life ebbs out,
> Will ride in a flaming chariot,
> Seated in state
> On a red-hot plate
> 'Twixt Satan and Judas Iscariot.[5]

These tales of a grandfather surged back in memory when one day in formal black attire I too found myself in St. Margaret's at the memorial service for some worthy and much decorated citizen. Up to the lectern proceeded the Right Honourable Harold Macmillan to read in his plummy voice that plummy passage about famous men. 'And their name liveth for ever' rolled out *Ecclesiastes* as mind wandered over Whitehall experiences from 1957 to 1961, recalled bland ambiguities on the margins of state papers, false jollities across the broad

[5] Quoted by Trevor Wilson, *The Downfall of the Liberal Party* (Fontana Library, 1968).

table at Number Ten, uneasy glances between other Ministers of the Crown, and the too easily overlooked assurances to foreign statesmen, or even worse, to spokesmen of distant tribes and peoples who had always looked to Britain but of whom apparently we knew nothing and cared even less. And it all ended in the Profumo debate with Mr. Nigel Birch quoting Browning's 'Lost Leader' while Mr. Macmillan dabbed away the suddenly welling tears.

Political leaders are always tempted to promise more than can be achieved. Now they run out of cake long before they have finished promising. They have not had an easy ride. Given the basic shift in Great Power alignments, the rise and fall of old and new states, the readjustments of wealth and influence within Western societies, there was bound to be even greater discrepancy between promise and fulfilment in the post-1945 world. The capacity for deception, which is firmly rooted in nature's order from the lowest to the highest form of life, could hardly fail to be put to use in the interests of human ambition. Referred to as a compromise between ideals and reality, it can be readily justified in academic essays, newspaper leaders, or Anglican sermons. But in more than one Western European state an intuitive point seems to have been reached when at any one time the vast majority of subjects feel betrayed over major national issues. Because their governments are sensed as being arbitrary, national obedience, that last ditch against anarchy and defeat, can no longer be unquestioning.

The dilemmas of rule are often crude and cruel and sufficient of older habits of governance still survive for us to be able to sense the predicaments of the rulers. Our contemporary emperors and popes can even demonstrate what was involved in the Latin of the palimpsests and help us to decide whether things are better or worse. And at close range the 'things' are not particularly attractive. Even after twelve months of coping with the deviousness and cruelty of the Amhara, it was in 1942 a shock to come up against imperial intrigue. The old game still went on. The patriot leader, Bilatta Takele, appointed by the Emperor as first Governor of Addis Ababa after its liberation, had proved a helpful soul during the concluding stages of the campaign against the Italians. Too helpful, it would seem, because as the last British forces evacuated the Abyssinian capital, he was arrested and was last seen on a lorry under armed guard being carried away to some fortress. At a later date he must have escaped because after more than two decades I read that someone of the same name had been killed by imperial troops in bush fighting. Takele had had the misfortune to have been one of the Abyssinians who during the Fascist occupation had actually kept an armed band in being so that a portion of Mussolini's empire remained unmapped, marked on Italian General Staff maps as *regioni infesti da ribelli*.

Here was a land with a feudal system which had survived beyond its *raison d'être*, a society without hope, without purpose, without loyalty, and which knew only doubt, betrayal, and fear. Even those aspects which give Abyssinian life its surface attraction, the handsome Semitic features of the Amhara, the ceremonies, the ranks and grades of nobility, priests and scribes, the robes and costumes, the games of the flower-bedecked children, and the beauty of the mountains serve by contrast to underline the strain of cruelty and treachery which runs from lowest subject to the ruler. Notions of tribal welfare which exist elsewhere in Africa are absent, intrigue and denunciation are the methods of advancement, and in this setting the symbols of a degenerate Christian cult reek of blasphemy. During the Italian period a few Abyssinians like Takele showed a somewhat unexpected loyalty to the exiled Emperor: the distant notion may have evoked something in them which the man did not. After the restoration these became the men to be feared perhaps because they seemed to possess a quality which others lacked, so that one by one they were destroyed.

One of the last was a capable little Armenian, who under the Fascist regime had maintained tenuous links between 'patriot' bands and friendly consulates. Entering his house one night, Johannes Semerdjibashian went down under a hail of fire from every conceivable small arm, including mortars, and the Abyssinian police neither knew nor wished to know anything about it. Finally in 1962 the hand-picked Imperial Guard turned against the Emperor during his absence on a state visit to Brazil, deposed him in favour of the Crown Prince and only the intervention of the mercenary troops of the regular army restored the situation. And up went the gallows in the main towns. 'But we were like that in the Middle Ages,' chirrup the European defenders of Abyssinian ways. Perhaps they see the sort of roles *they* would have liked to play in the Middle Ages.

But the king was originally the 'cunning one'. Success in wielding power is the ultimate test of a ruler's ability and 'weak' monarchs get no approbation from history. Where loyalty has died, calculation must take its place. Of the world's other two contemporary emperors, the occupant of the Peacock Throne and Centre of the Universe, the Shahinshah of Iran, may not have to cope with the crudities of

Abyssinia, but the very subtleties and refinement of the tapestry of Iranian civilization require from him a correspondingly sophisticated assessment of the threats to his rule and of the needs and methods of power.

As a boy he had suddenly been put on the throne by British and Russians after a respected though domineering father had been sent into exile. In 1953 he had been briefly dethroned by Mussadeq. In 1955, when I was first given a private audience, he was uncertain of the extent of outside influence and intrigue among his subjects, and faced by strong tribal chiefs, by generals of uncertain loyalty, and by cross-streams of popular and religious resentment. Now he is monarch of all he surveys; as he remarked: 'The British and American ambassadors used to tell me that I must not get immersed in the details of government. As a constitutional monarch I should behave like an institution and keep my head in the clouds. And then one day I found myself in Rome with a few thousand lira and a republic declared in Teheran. When I came back I resolved that this would never happen again and from now on I would rule myself.'

So the generals were played off against each other and thrown out. The tribes were quietened, the foreign oil interests are totally without political influence, the imams confine themselves to the holy texts, women are unveiled and possess the vote while the whole Iranian people are advancing in terms of material welfare. Part of the process may have been successful 'intrigue'. But the Centre of the Universe knows that he can maintain himself only so long as he enjoys the trust of sufficient of his people and that he must return this trust. His enemies may attack him as greedy and vindictive and the Iranian national sport has been described as kicking a man when he is down. If he kicked all of them all of the time this could prove a ruler's undoing. But a few years ago the Shah did get rid of the security chief who was alleged to use a wild bear as a technique for interrogating troublesome students. 'And it's part of my job', he said, 'to be shot at by assassins.' So far he remains on top.

And for popes the problem remains of how to deal with the conflicting pressures of secular rulers while maintaining the credibility of the institution as a focus of faith and loyalty. It is no easier for them to-day than with their mediæval and Renaissance predecessors. My first encounter with Pope Paul VI illustrated the predicament although he wasn't pope—yet. For it was only July 1944 and it had occurred to some high-up in the Allied war effort that through the clergy in German-occupied Europe the Vatican must possess an extensive

B

knowledge of the identities of Gestapo and SS. personnel, particularly those concerned with mass arrests and extermination. The Polish Resistance in particular had emphasized that if the names of such Nazi officials were broadcast by the B.B.C. with appropriate warnings as to their post-war fate, life became at least marginally easier for those over whom they had the power of life and death. Life even reappeared as a possibility for some of the victims.

Could discreet contact be made with the Vatican? Nothing easier! We got hold of Monsignor O'Flaherty who up to the Allied arrival in Rome had run a most successful escape and evasion line for British prisoners of war. 'It's a difficult one, me bhoy,' he said. 'It's a matter for Monsignor Montini. I'll bring him along.' So we met the man who is now Pope Paul. We didn't expect him to give us the German Army order of battle. It was a question of trying to halt human suffering and saving innocent lives—many of them members of his own cult. He listened, one cannot say impassively, but with his priest's face—that semi-smile without laughter he still has. And commented rightly enough that it was a matter for his superiors to decide. They did. Some days later O'Flaherty came back—alone. 'I'm sorry, me bhoy,' he said. 'There's nothing doing.'

After nearly twenty years I saw Monsignor Montini again. On entering an Italian bank I had not expected to run into a cardinal-archbishop in full canonicals with thurifers out in front and a procession of Milanese dignatories in the rear. Cardinal Montini had been blessing the statue of St. Ambrosius on the main staircase. As a humble spectator I received my share of the benediction bestowed by the two upraised fingers. And on his face the same smile which is not a smile.

One can hear all the arguments against the 1944 proposition. Vengeance is mine, saith the Lord. Life is but a vale of tears for us all. And are the British secure anyway? As far as the last point is concerned George Blake has answered their prayers and justified their caution so that Pope Paul can now say: 'If I hadn't played that one cool, I might never have been able to issue *De Humanae Vitae*.' Betrayed humanity marched to the gas ovens but at the time the credibility of the institution seemed to have been preserved. It has subsequently proved to be the issue which has brought greatest discredit on the Vatican.

While the acts of Haile Selassie and Pope Paul can be set in a feudal perspective and contemporary Polish, Hungarian, and Czech leaders have suffered the same fate as John Huss trusting his imperial safe-conduct to Constance, only a cartoonist can put Messrs. Harold

Macmillan and Harold Wilson in gothic attitudes and stiff-hanging robes of state. Here loyalty and betrayal are of another order. Nor do Thorneycroft, Powell, Birch, Watkinson and Selwyn Lloyd quite fit the role of disconsolate vassals being led in chains off the tapestry. But in some ways the sense of loyalty of electorate and party workers was outraged by these two Prime Ministers. This was no question of material expectations left unfulfilled: the sense of being let down went further. In both cases the Harolds fell into the same trap as Lloyd George.

'The man who enters public life at this epoch', wrote Disraeli in *Coningsby*, 'has to chose between Political Infidelity and a Destructive Creed.' But whatever intrigue, double-dealing and dishonesty persisted among British Parliamentary leaders and factions before 1900, they had not to cope with a widely read popular daily Press. When some monkey-business was afoot, those who suspected or were in the know, such as editors and constituency chiefs, rather revelled in such goings-on for their own sake. It gave them a sense of sharing in the process of power which all men love, while up to 1900 or thereabouts the belief prevailed that the Press could be bought up or managed. So it could —and so it can—but not all of it all of the time.

The misjudgement seems to have resulted in great part from the lack of a sense of the fitting. 'Lloyd George suddenly turned round and said: "Bonar, I think that you know that you are different from most of us because you are a man who would act on principle: if you thought a thing was right you would do it." Bonar replied: "Well, I think it's my Covenanting blood." And then Lloyd George grinned across at me and turned and grinned at Bonar and said: "Bonar, you know, I can conceive of circumstances arising in which I might be compelled to act on principle myself—but you can't say that of F.E. [F. E. Smith, later Lord Birkenhead] or Winston, can you?" '[6] Although crowds still turned out to see 'the man who had won the war', Lloyd George went down and out of effective policy-making. Churchill came back because he was less unprincipled than largely motivated by the instincts and prejudices shared by the majority of his fellow-countrymen—an Alf Garnett writ large and as such taken to the people's hearts in time of doubt and danger.

Baldwin's merit was that he gave Britain back the illusion that it

[6] *Memoirs of a Conservative.* J. C. C. Davidson's Memoirs and Papers 1910-1937 (Weidenfeld & Nicolson, 1969).

had again leaders who deserved some trust. Although announcing as his basic precept 'When in doubt, choose the path you like least', in practice he followed the national habit of evading the issue, of ducking it altogether and vanishing to his constituency, to Aix-lès-Bains, or to some ceremonial occasion where he presided admirably, coming back when the crisis was over and had been resolved by others. But since he was never seen to be conducting intrigues, led a blameless personal life, and as an individual—as I found myself—extremely kind, he met the mood of the nation which was not one of grasping nettles.

Was he the cunning one? Or was it instinct? Even his closest political confidant could never be sure and would only comment: 'He really is a most extraordinary man.' And this was the same mantle assumed by Attlee in the quiet times after the Churchillian years, with a similar description of 'a most remarkable man' from his former Cabinet colleagues, as they recall how round the table at Number Ten his reaction to some critical question facing the post-war Labour Government was: 'Have you seen Low's cartoon to-day?' He had the same facility as Baldwin for being inaccessible at times of decision, as with the Schuman Plan and Abadan when in the case of the former we renounced the role of leadership in Western Europe and with the second abandoned our Middle Eastern position of ascendancy.

So it is interesting that national suspicion has settled on Macmillan and Wilson as the two main passers of political counterfeit. For in practice Attlee was narrow-minded and spiteful. Churchill could be cavalier with truth. Eden grew increasingly irritable and Douglas-Home's *sancta simplicitas* misled him on more than one occasion as to where lay the national interest. On quitting office they left the electorate with a sense of unfulfilled expectation but not with resentful feelings of betrayal. In spite of anathema maranatha from Anglican bishops and Left-Wing intellectuals at the 'immorality' of the 1956 Suez expedition, the popular view was that Eden had tried to do the right thing but had made a mess of it—a pretty accurate assessment of what actually did happen. And now Eden enjoys something of the reputation of a respected elder statesman whereas the Macmillan years are increasingly regarded by politicos, civil servants, allies and by the mass of the nation as a time of let-down.

An unfair suspicion? As new volumes appear of his own memoirs and of those of foreign statesmen, the impression is heightened. Who was the 'real' Macmillan—the young Tory reformer of the thirties, the wartime diplomat with his too-clever-by-half pen sketches of Allied commanders (mostly decent men confronted by problems without precedent) or the insincere ageing charmer of post-war governments? His Premiership was remarkable in the atmosphere of mistrust he created round him. Even the long historical disquisitions began to be regarded as some form of a deception gambit. The amusing game of playing one Minister off against another was extended to foreign governments who would be invited by the angled question to give the answer which would stymie domestic proposals by his own Cabinet colleagues. The British officials who were used as instruments in this game rapidly sensed how best to qualify for preferment. The Downing Street toadies made sure that none of them would be the bearer of bad tidings. The Secretary of the Cabinet somehow omitted to pass on the papers on the Profumo affair when a friendly admonition could have put it all straight. And when the time came to play the 'good butcher' —a role described in the Macmillan 'Memoirs' as an essential quality in a Prime Minister—he made an unholy mess. On Civil Service Selection Boards I had often expressed the view that if presented with the problem of murdering their grandmother, Etonians would either do the job brilliantly or botch it completely with blood all round the room and Grandma still breathing.

How does a Prime Minister become set on a course which can only end in universal mistrust? And why should Wilson have picked up the moth-eaten *tarnkappe* of Lloyd George after Macmillan had let it fall? His victims seemed a pathetic lot—Brown, Gordon Walker, Bottomley, Bowden, Wigg, Willey, Gunter, and Jay. There seemed no reason for sacrificing them except to demonstrate his dexterity. The Archbishop of Canterbury realized too late that he had been lured into demonstrating along with his 'National' Committee for Commonwealth Immigrants that he was impotent to enforce what he had preached on the subject of racial integration. Frank Cousins, after having professed the doctrine of the brotherhood of man, was asked to prove it by forcing the same coloured men on to unwilling trade unionists. Having advocated one per cent of the gross national product as Britain's contribution to backward peoples, Mrs. Barbara Castle was given the task of cutting aid for the underdeveloped. The lavishing of honours on pop singers, negro comedians, and the current stars of the entertainment world resembled nothing so much as Byzantine emperors placating the Blues and Greens of the hippodrome. There was obviously no place for idealistic simpletons such as Mr. Christopher Mayhew.

As a style of government it may have been a more civilized method of incapacitating one's potential challengers than blinding or castrating them. But in Wilson's case it coincided with the greatest non-fulfilment of British political expectations in the post-War World. Wilson's speech of 14th April 1965 to the Economic Club of New York was probably the high point of promise when he described his farsighted economic plans and Britain's biggest peacetime revolution in the machinery of government. The panic reversals of policy in 1966 showed that in fact Wilson had foreseen nothing. As with Lloyd George an attempt was made to build up influence by patronage with an assortment of Tory renegades, businessmen avid for knighthoods and peerages, while boards, councils, corporations and commissions were created to fill up an empty shop window. By 1969 Wilson had lost all credibility and, when the election came, attempts to present a new statesmanlike image failed because of his own inability to rise above what his opponents called his alley-cat technique.

It was a failure where loyalty suffered. Inside the political process the active participants may be allowed a certain cynicism about each other's motives. But for the country at large this can never be enough. The art of the possible requires from the artist a generally acceptable style. There is therefore a limit to the type of compromise which can be effected between ideals and reality. Political deception to-day also involves a new factor. In Europe's past, the response of subjects for whom the sense of betrayal had become intolerable was revolt, war, or conspiracy. Their 'right' to do so seems to have been conceded early in the feudal age and was founded in the last analysis on the sufficiency of their means for successful revolt.

But now those who are betrayed are expected to join publicly in maintaining the deception. While unseated politicians who hope to make a comeback can no doubt fall in with the rules of this game, it is asking a good deal of the generality that they should identify themselves with disloyalty and still remain loyal, that they should support the self-deception of ministers by lying to themselves. The politics of sado-masochism even require the betrayer to demand that society punish itself to expiate his betrayal. Mr. Quintin Hogg, now serving his second term as Lord Hailsham, is one of the arch-exponents: 'You are all to blame', he cries whenever the electorate shows signs of reacting against the neglect and dereliction of duty by those who hold or have held office. On the Labour side, Mr. Roy Hattersley put the same point: 'It is all too easy to believe that new men with new policies could put the country right painlessly and quickly.'[7] But this was precisely what he and his colleagues had wanted us to believe. So! In Tory and Labour orthodoxy it had become disloyal to draw attention to disloyalty.

An established style of rule which consists of avoiding difficult decisions or action by playing off disparate elements against each other will not be changed overnight. It is a situation where, to use David Riesman's phrase in *The Lonely Crowd*,[8] 'Power is dispersed among veto groups.' 'Bi-partisan politics', the favourite nostrum of those who write to the newspapers expressing disgust with the main parties, will only make this situation worse. Indeed much of the electorate's disbelief and resentments in the early sixties arose from the bi-partisan plot to keep issues such as race from being openly discussed, and the gap between governors and governed was on the point of becoming unbridgeable until Powell brought this particular question out into the open. The passions of a people must find expression and statesmen have to assist in this as well as find compromises. When no one believes in an exclusion, it can no longer be maintained. The Liberal Party probably began its decline when those it excluded or pretended did not exist—Irish nationalists, trade-union militants, and suffragettes—managed to make their physical presence felt.

So it is not a question of whether 'democracy could survive another battering of the kind it has received from Labour', as Mr. Edward Heath put it.[9] Can he and his colleagues reverse the continual discrediting of our political institutions from Lloyd George to Wilson? Society may need Ibsen's 'saving lies'—the dissembling and hypocrisy which soften human asperities and which are derived from 'received values'. But it cannot exist entirely off mistrust. If we could count on no national crisis ever arising as a result of internal upheaval or external pressures, each of us might hope to retire into our personal selfishness and allow advancing material welfare to take care of general stability or social peace. In theory, the doped society which needs neither liege nor lord may seem possible.

In practice this does not happen. Those elements most subject to commercial dope of one kind or another have not only become sedative-resistant but positively violent. Under present circumstances,

[7] Address to Young Socialists, 15.9.68.
[8] Yale University Press, 1950.
[9] Annual Conservative Party Conference, 1968.

major racial conflict seems likely before the end of the seventies and certainly in the decade following. It would be a brave man who would prophesy that Britain will not within a generation be faced with external threats to its survival as menacing and as unforeseen as was Naziism. At such a point a leadership which can command loyalty will be required. And this leadership will have to draw on the social style under which its members grew up and acquired office; for their appeal as leaders will in practice be a more emphatic form of this style. Stalin could never abandon the conspiratorial mode nor Roosevelt the genial demagoguery of American pork-barrel politics. Churchill retained his imperial horizons and De Gaulle the abstract logic of the *haute école de guerre*. Seen realistically Britain will for a decade or longer have to draw its political leadership from men who were trained to run after events. They may yet master them and such is always the promise of a new administration. But the first fanfares of departmental reorganization prove so often to have been substitutes for the policies they were supposed to implement, and the inertia of the governmental machine permits only limited fringe domestic initiatives which usually harry the more defenceless members of society. And since the sixties, Britain has been unable to influence the major policy decisions of other states so that the limits of our defence position, our economy, and of our technology have been determined by circumstances outside our volition. This has had its impact throughout the whole machinery of administration and on the outward style of government.

Every election produces its new contingent of M.P.s who—we are assured by the lobby correspondents—will create a new Parliamentary ethos. After two years one hears little more about them and when one eventually rises to being Under-Secretary for Ag and Fish he behaves very much like the predecessors who were pushed on or out. The Monday Club diligently plans its pressure tactics to influence the course of Tory policies and while it has certainly been successful in changing the tone of the leaders' speeches, the House of Commons itself can only follow behind the events as interpreted to them by Ministers. The weight of Parliamentary business will keep it basically a rubber-stamping instrument—from 272 pages of laws in 1900 to 2,207 in 1967 and still rising. This is a far cry from Palmerston's response in 1864 to the question of what would be his legislative programme for next session: 'Oh! There's really nothing to be done. We cannot go on adding to the Statute Book *ad infinitum*.'

And there is no non-Parliamentary 'Establishment' such as existed in all its glory before 1914 and gradually faded into obscurity if not disrepute during the twenties and thirties. Even though Britain has gone through the greatest defence reappraisal since the pre-1914 introduction of the dreadnoughts, the three forces have failed to throw up any service chief with the temperament of Admiral Lord Fisher whose intense sense of duty transmuted itself into a need for mastery. Few Ministers, much less M.P.s and electors, can even name the heads of the armed services. There is no corps of grandees with a tradition of vice-regal or pro-consular service, only the tall amiable ones round their high tables grumbling that the Somalis or Rhodesians or others will not lie down and keep quiet so that their own petty betrayals can be decently buried. In the City establishment, Sir Leslie O'Brien's rather colourless tenure of the Governorship of the Bank of England meets the requirements of the age more aptly than the neurotic dicta-torialism of Montagu Norman would have done. The odd banker, industrialist, or trade unionist flits in and out of a national board or corporation without the nation at large identifying itself with his rise and fall.

The general tenor of the Fulton Report of 1968 on civil-service reform was in fact that élites are out of place and administrative efficiency is everything.[10] Unfortunately it does not work out like that since industries, for example, are nationalized and denationalized for political motives and not for economic reasons, so that civil servants have still to work out politically acceptable ways of doing so: they are still concerned with power. The consequences of the Robbins Report advocating an accelerated expansion of high educational institutions have been to lower the standard of teaching in those subjects on which we are told—rightly or wrongly—our national survival depends. Further recruitment of non-classical and non-literary civil-service candidates, as advocated by Fulton, could take away even more of a dwindling cream so that the final outcome may be a markedly inferior top administrative layer in government. We are caught in a process of erosion of the human elements on whom depends the effective wielding of power; so even more could events take their course.

Can 'organized' labour provide an establishment with a broad command of loyalties? The years of full employment certainly presented new possibilities of power which were grasped and used to the full by

[10] The Civil Service: Report of the Committee. 1966–8 Cmd. 3638.

Swedish, German, Austrian, and some other European trade unions. Yet the nominal British trade-union leaders were hesitant to assume similar responsibilities, largely, it would appear, lest from one side they were accused of compounding with the employers and to the other exposed as incapable of asserting authority over rank and file. Industrial legislation, whether proposed by a Labour or a Conservative Government, which would have given the Trades Union Congress leadership legal authority to bolster its waning power, has been hotly opposed so that real authority rests with shop-floor leaders cashing in on the resentful agin-the-boss solidarity left over from battles long ago. The dialogue between the union leaders and politicians of all parties thus remains an ill-defined discussion on the proper use of the power of the state over both employers and workers. Here is no marriage of function and loyalty.

At best the gestures of solidarity—however spasmodic—do maintain loyalties on a human level. The British dockers, who enjoy a public image of passionate rebels ready to respond to any rabble-rouser, prove on closer acquaintance to be taking their strikes rather lightly— often too lightly as they later discover—and treated their Jack Dash as a favourite comedy act. Provided they do not feel that they are breaking faith with each other, they cheerfully accept irrational compromises and illogical settlements. And to the confusion of the Programme Three dons who contribute to *New Society*, *New Statesman*, *New Scientist*, and similar passing shows, the same dockers are passionate admirers of both Jack Dash and Enoch Powell. So much so that the problem is not the Old Adam—he is perfectly explicable—but rather those who refuse to admit his existence after the clear evidence of a million years of human evolution.

The one-time lower orders are in reality utterly different from the notion of a working class adumbrated from Blanqui, Marx, to the progressive sociologists and 'revolutionary' students of to-day. The average male Briton who has spent part, and usually the observant and receptive part, of his life clumping around in army boots in various regions of the world, coming off tramp steamers in strange ports, or mining in Asia, Africa, and the Andes, has a vast fund of experience of the apparently contradictory realities of human existence. Bloggs' views on the wogs are not to be dismissed as 'prejudice' even in a British social context. It is the dogmatic fallacies about society which are irrelevant. 'Morality', whatever the moralists may advocate, is still no more than the *mores* of human beings. The concept of idle leisure is not an appealing one to the working class nor is it a true one. The workaday world needs a sense of unity of both work and purpose. And at times of national survival it is Private Bloggs who has to cope with basic Man as he meets him on the battlefield and other rough-and-tumble situations, not someone like Mr. Harold Wilson sitting in a wartime Whitehall ministry producing well-turned memoranda.

The cynicism of political office-holders and their permanent servants, by which for the last fifty years they have treated ideas as little more than stage props for their Westminster and Whitehall acts, finds its counterpart among the audience which may be naïve in expression but is by no means simple. Most of the electorate remain somewhat detached about our political institutions whatever lip service they hear being paid to them. This is in great part because the stratification sustained by the peculiarly English types of snobbery built into the educational system has insulated from intellectual malaise those whom older aristocrats and newer sociologists persist in treating as 'masses', and also because at least one generation accepts that there is no inherent good in a political system which tolerated mass unemployment at home and compromises with Naziism abroad. They easily take in their stride similar 'compromises' about the Commonwealth and the United Nations.

But there is a gap which has to be bridged and so far patriotism is the major residual loyalty which does so. This is still powerful even among the young—as the Monday Club has found out to its gratification—who comprise a surprising number of romantics combining love of country with a preference for being clean rather than dirty and who like their girl friends washed as well. A poll of young men in 1970 found a third ready to be conscripted to fight for Queen and Country and another third ready to perform some type of national service. But patriotism too depends on the existence of a corporate image of ourselves as being something better than we know ourselves to be as individuals. The monarch helped us along so long as we could convincingly project our fantasies about ourselves on to him or her. Now royalty appears to have chosen to destroy its own magic doubtless in the belief that this will bring it closer to the people. But, alas, a gesture of loyalty is not easy to make towards those who are patently no better than we are. The daily photograph of minor royalties and their associates seems to turn the most romantic Jacobite into a raving Jacobin.

Up to the seventeenth century, monarchs contrived to embody what most of their subjects were prepared to accept as a 'national interest' although it was frequently only the ruler's own interest expressed as an antagonism towards other rulers and peoples. In the eighteenth century, Parliament was still largely concerned with domestic affairs so that both Whig oligarchs and the nominees of Tory grandees could put across with convincing sincerity their notions of national goals, reflecting the rise of groups and classes sufficiently disinterested to stand above the mundane pressures of daily necessity. The advent of Victorian political oratory with its moralizing quality, the growth of paternalistic social legislation and a widely sensed pride in country and empire had by 1914 heightened the illusion of a common cause and an interest which was both national and genuinely popular. Even the 'radicals' and the new working-class leadership who attacked imperialism profited from this sense of loyal emotion in putting across their own version of historical destiny and common weal.

And sadly one comes back to Lloyd George as the main trickster of our century. Sadly, because he was the first politician of modern times to have evoked the full force of patriotism—and how superbly he did it—in British society as a whole. Perhaps it could have only one genuine evocation because thereafter the tricks were as inevitable as the sense of let-down. Since his time those who form coalitions to defend a national interest are liable to be denounced as traitors even though their attackers may be motivated solely by resentment at the loss of office or preferment. Nevertheless the attacks find a response: coalition and consensus are suspected by the electorate of being cover for conspiracy.

The heightened self-consciousness of to-day means that society cannot accept certain forms of degradation in its midst any more than it could suffer a reintroduction of torture into the judicial process. A Parliament of weak corrupt men may have offered certain advantages in George III's time if it enabled his Ministers to manage the Commons without undue worry while they concentrated on matters which seemed to them of more concern than county privilege. But in 1940 when the Commons was for once called to speak and act for the nation, such a state of affairs could have been a national disaster.

To survive, institutions must not only be effective. They must be seen to be deriving their quality from those who embody them. Their debasement affects the character of the people and their dis-appearance without replacement endangers identity. Here the Scots are a warning. Their own political institutions never recovered fully from their rough handling by Cromwell and the Scottish Estates re-emerged as a cabal of aristocratic patrons manipulating sycophantic hangers-on from the burghs. The outcome of being unable to act politically as Scots has been a nation at once whining for alms and then cursing the giver. After the loss of the Scottish Parliament even a separate church and a further century of vigorous intellectual life were not enough.

For a community which wishes to survive as such has still to maintain itself against external pressures and influences. Suggestions that we can with equanimity allow politics to sink to the level of a second-order entertainment need careful examination. How long can general scepticism and individual greed and ambition sustain the common assumptions on which institutions depend? Will the gap not become unbridgeable? The history of the Third and Fourth French Republics provides the unambiguous answer that without a sense of national participation in common purpose and a clearly defined accountability of the governing group to the governed, disintegration is the result or an outsider moves in.

In less self-conscious days old forms could be restored. European kingship underwent severe setbacks after the end of the Carolingian era but revived vigorously under Capets, Plantagenets and Hohenstaufens. The fiefs of vassals, the tenements and allods of farmers, the guaranteed charters and privileges of merchants and guilds provided such a solid foundation of interest that even a discredited dynasty or council could use it to renew the basis of authority. But where nominal privilege is diffused, as in the case of democracies whose ultimate authority is the mythical abstraction of a freedom-loving and altruistic Man, and material bonds of interest are less obvious, it may need external threats to restore common loyalty. And even that may be disputed or denounced as 'artificial' or 'emotional' by those whose material interests do not seem to be under immediate threat, or who fear the new consolidation of power which revived loyalties would bring about.

Every European nation-state preserves the embodiments, the residues, and the resentments of all these past dispersals and reconsolidations. And now a new factor is the unprecedented acceleration of social change. Although Europeans are geared to change in their environment and can absorb most of its effects provided their emotional lives are sufficiently stable, the time-span of major change is now considerably shorter than that of the normal human span. The unknown now irrupts in unexpected forms several times within a generation.

In the past the welding force was usually violence. 'And as wars in some sort may be said to be a ravisher, so it cannot be denied but peace is a great maker of cuckolds. Ay, and it makes men hate one another. Reason: because they then less need one another. The wars for my money.'[11] Long before Shakespeare the same sentiments had been expressed: 'I love the gay Eastertide which brings forth leaves and flowers; and I love the joyous songs of the birds re-echoing through the copse. But also I love to see, amidst the meadows, tents and pavilions spread: and it gives me great joy to see, drawn up on the field, knights and horses in battle array; and it delights me when the scouts scatter people and herds in their path; and I love to see them followed by a great body of men-at-arms; and my heart is filled with gladness when I see strong castles besieged, and the stockades broken and overwhelmed and the warriors on the bank, girt about by fosses, with a line of strong stakes interlaced . . . Maces, swords, helms of different hues, shields that will be riven and shattered as soon as the fight begins: and many vassals struck down together; and the horses of the dead and the wounded roving at random. And when battle is joined let all men of good lineage think of naught but the breaking of heads and arms: for it is better to die than to be vanquished and live.'[12]

Violence is not lacking to-day. Not only the criminal variety but an aimless resort to blind action where at least a sort of animal allegiance is established. Our latter-day 'parceners of the ragged cloak', the rootless writers and academics who occupy so much of the written and spoken media of the Western world, find intellectual justification for this. Since they feel themselves among the Philistines, the temple might as well come down. And when acts of government are sensed to be increasingly arbitrary, the self-assertive reaction will be arbitrary violence, and not only among racial groups, football supporters, and criminal elements. If there is a growing desire to hurt and torture we shall also see a spread of masochistic breast-beating where the most dissatisfied will be the so-called emancipated.

Will the residual loyalties inherited by Western Europe from its older history be sufficient for our society to hold up under these strains? Patriotism can rally the majority of the descendants of those who have been indigenous to these islands since 1066 or thereabouts, or have

[11] *Coriolanus.* Act IV, Scene 5.
[12] Twelfth-century *troubadour*, probably Bertrand de Borne. Quoted by Marc Bloch, *Feudal Society* (Routledge & Kegan Paul, 1961), p. 293.

subsequently arrived in small enough numbers and from cultures cognate enough to enable their offspring to identify with the rest of the British nations. But the margin narrows and only when it is too late will it be found to have reached vanishing point. The failure of any group to meet a challenge brings in its trail rancour and yet more violence. The 'collaborator' after defeat is notoriously more vicious than the occupier and doubtless an invader would to-day have an easier task than in 1940 in finding all the quislings he needed between Smith Square and Throgmorton Street.

Resentment is a powerful force. Men's jackal strain—developed during their first 600,000 years as a separate species—emerges quickly enough among those suffering from a sense of inadequacy and the heart rejoices when it sees some other creature beginning to falter and stumble: the pack will be on it soon enough. Subliminated as morality, the need for scapegoats becomes overweening and custom too is turned into arbitrariness. This seems to have been the case in the unhappy centuries when under irruptions of Norsemen and Magyars, kinship collapsed in feud and jealousy. However at some point in time resentment does turn back against the perpetrators of violence and the need for a common focus of authority and loyalty returns—as often as not to the benefit of the invaders. The arbitrariness of baronial rule and of the courts of local magnates and counts in the age of feudal decay caused men to turn to the king's peace—any king's—so that 'under him we may be godly and quietly governed' as the Anglican Communion puts it.

The danger of civil conflict of which Mr. Edward Heath warned the United Nations General Assembly is already one which confronts that symbol of the Western world's outward striving, the New Found Land which revived old idealisms. In spite of their disparate origins, the varied groups forming the people of the United States developed a unique loyalty to the American dream, symbolized sometimes by the flag, by a President, by a cause, or by the hope of victory. When the dream is finally seen to be unrealizable, what happens to a people so inclined to over-react? What scapegoats will have to be turned out to satisfy their frustrations? In the self-confident America of the twenties the scattered wrecks of old cars which heralded the proximity of yet another 'Greatest Little City' of the Middle West (or West) suggested that the nation's custom was then to load all its sins on last year's model and send it careering out into the prairie to perish. But now barricades, moral or physical, have to be manned—and stormed.

The year 1969 was probably the climactic intensification of the crisis of disbelief—the Fortas case, the Pueblo naval inquiry, the trial of Martin Luther King's killer, and a new spread of conflict to be followed in 1970 by a general acceptance that the future would be one of domestic violence. Some of the moral myths of 1776 have died.

So the dice are loaded against the restoration of old authorities which will command old loyalties. We have to abandon regrets for the past and consider what it has left us in the way of consequences. It may then be possible to identify the course of action. Confusing though the path of British politics may be between 1920 and the present day, Lloyd George's pragmatism and cunning have meant that we have never been faced by some of the worst consequences of parties wedded to exalted principles. Because there were no clearly defined idealist alignments and the Parliamentary institutions continued to work, Labour was able to introduce peacefully its post-World War Two programme. But, since insincerity and treachery are built into the tactics for winning and holding office, Parliamentary groups have taken on the same hue. Since new 'ideals' or new totems cannot be effectively set up inside the system, small extremist groups in the Commons can never create a new political 'climate' in either Parliament or country. And our psephologists expend quite a mental effort and an extraordinary number of words to establish the obvious, that social stratification and the general acceptance that no promise of Utopia is realizable can have no other outcome than the creation of a sceptical floating vote, while politicians will turn to scapegoat hunting in place of causes.

Can we identify any factors analogous to those which created the fealties of the early Middle Ages and ultimately brought about the powerful loyalties of the states of nineteenth-century Europe? The collision of two different social structures—one based on kinship, the other on the administrative hierarchic system of the Western Roman Empire—created the need for a new ordering principle with both invaders and invaded. The very violence of the times—whether the external threat of Norsemen, Magyars, and Arabs, or the internal conflicts of power and ambition—became the welding force for the human relationships which were later ordered into a society of fiefs and tenements. Enough of the Roman institutions and the scribes to operate them remained to provide the new order with the conceptual framework which later became its claim to legitimacy.

Older elements of pre-Roman life left their residue—the community sense of Bronze-Age manorial groupings, the myths of Celtic chieftainship which in North-West Scotland remained the strongest binding force up to mid-eighteenth century, and the pledges and promises of the merchant colonies of the Mediterranean ports and the plains and valleys of the Po, Rhone, Rhine and Danube. In history there are no breaks—these exist only in the minds of scribes when the documents are missing. The bill of exchange—mankind's oldest written pledge—is torn up once it is honoured but the trust on which it was based lives on in the consciousness of men. And the embodiment of trust as a formal loyalty requires the effectiveness of rule. 'Considered historically the state had been primary everywhere in Europe and the nation the product of living conditions within the limits of a certain state. The nation had formed itself only within the context of authority.'[13]

So to establish a new authority and to distinguish between loyalty and betrayal, society's scheme of things must concede to power its recognized role. A people's identification of community, creed, or language—for weal or for woe—can never be assured without a focus of power. It is central to any process of re-identification. The contemporary world has paid a high price for the nineteenth-century liberal's rejection of power as being a mere corruption, and his attempt to replace it by higher principles such as 'freedom', 'tolerance', 'legitimacy', 'human dignity', and 'social justice'. Lenin and Hitler saw through the liberal fallacy: the latter in particular grasped that the effective exercise of power creates its own loyalties and common interests. In our time it has taken less than a decade for the new rulers of Africa to divest themselves of the intellectual rags and tatters picked up in French and British colleges, so that they now blatantly play the role of 'cunning ones' even when not formally installed as kings. *Kunst macht Gunst*: the strong can enjoy his own again. The Shah commands loyalty because he wields effective power: the papacy loses credibility as it becomes only too apparent that Pope Paul cannot send one recusant priest to the stake. The raggle-taggle groups who emerge with cries of 'Black Power' and 'Student Power' have at least sensed that here is a vacuum to be filled.

But by itself cunning cannot be enough for the West: only in the Arab world is a man still considered 'good' because of his wealth, strength, or guile. Our consciousness has evolved in a setting of ideas

[13] J. H. Huizinga, *Men and Ideas* (Eyre & Spottiswoode, 1960), p. 138.

C

and unless ideas are sensed to be valid we shall feel unsure of our identity. Ideas which are no longer valid, i.e. have ceased to be accurate descriptions of human motives or of external reality, rapidly become topsy-turvy instruments of expediency. Nor can reversion to a separate morality for princes be reconciled with the evolutionary stage reached by other institutions of society: our courts must be seen to be impartial. A Western state run only by cunning might flounder along like the Third and Fourth French Republics until external defeat or the threat of internal anarchy produced an acceptable strong man. As in Central and Eastern Europe in the twenties and thirties, political gangsters can for a time play their little protection games until one day Arturo Ui sweeps them all into his bigger racket. British governments cannot forever disguise arbitrariness as legality, repress in the name of tolerance or declare self-defence to be provocation: at some point a Home Secretary would be regarded as little different from the Kray brothers. There would be no trustful response from the people.

Must we go through the anarchy of violence to find new loyalty? Recent cases of treason and also the phenomena of neo-anarchism are often described—and even defended on our State broadcasting system— as resulting from disgust against the 'system'. Does this stand up to close examination? By studying the nature of betrayal, of falsehood towards those who had given their trust, of disappointing human hopes and expectations, shall we find a path back to loyalty? When there is a sense of general let-down, so that even the petty deceptions of political lobbies, of constituency intrigues, of chairmen's assurances to share-holders, of employers to employees and vice versa begin to assume new and sinister aspects, were our traitors only in search of someone they could really trust? The plots, intrigues, espionage and eventually the civil wars of the Elizabethan and Stuart reigns are only explicable in the setting of the changing allegiances of English and Scottish monarchs over a century and a half. It was the people who were searching for an enduring loyalty in the face of fickle rulers.

But in contemporary Britain our nominal liege lords are ideas— freedom, democracy, justice, compassion! And it is noticeable that the patently destructive elements in our midst also claim to be acting in the name of these ideas. Outwardly the kiss of loyalty and the Judas version look much the same. If even kinship is a tale of hates and jealousies, can there be such a thing as treason? Are we betraying the ideas or are the ideas betraying us?

II. Flagellants or Funnies?

II. Flagellants or Funnies?

The argument that the betrayers were searching for a higher loyalty suggests that we can distill some common essence from the more notorious cases of treachery over the last two or three decades. Are spies our inner challenge to present and future?[1] But in the most publicised instances this remains not proven. William Joyce, who became Goebbel's Lord Haw-Haw, was unfortunate in picking the wrong passport out of the three to which he could have apparently laid claim: otherwise he would have escaped the gallows—a fascinating side-comment on the privileges and rights which may accrue to those to whom British passports are issued. Fuchs had never really belonged to any allegiance and some resentment at not belonging kept gnawing away inside him. For most of his life his need had been for a father confessor and when he finally succeeded by a most tortuous path in finding one, he inflicted a trying role on the Special Branch officer who had to cope with him: but it produced one of the most interesting psychological documents in Scotland Yard's records.

An even more far-fetched suggestion is that Maclean and Philby can be linked across a century and a half with the 'Napoleonist Syndrome'—those admirers of the French Revolution such as Charles James Fox, Byron, the Hollands, Hazlitt, and at the end of last century the pro-Boers such as Lloyd George.[2] The origins of the 'syndrome' are the inevitable despotic parents and the symptoms include, in addition to taking the side of one's country's current enemy, ambition, humanitarianism, addiction to animal pets, gift for foreign languages but a tendency to stutter. All very plausible unless one knows that

---

[1] '. . . a study of espionage, as suggested at the beginning of this book, confronts us with the true nature of our allegiances and of things we do not normally have to bring into the scales. Spies challenge us to decide what our attitude be towards events which do not seem likely to happen yet, but could happen.' Michael Burn, *The Debatable Land* (Hamish Hamilton, 1970), p. 256.
[2] E. Tangye Lean, *The Napoleonists: A Study in Political Disaffection 1760–1960* (O.U.P., 1970).

throughout Britain among serious integrated decent people there was
continuous widespread admiration for Napoleon's achievements in
the field of emancipation and reform and the hope that one day the
excesses of both French Revolution and Napoleonic conquests would
be rectified by the Emperor.[3]

But because of their school and university background, Maclean,
Burgess, and Philby do seem to fall into one category. Probably they
were talent-spotted by the same scout who operated for the Russian
secret service and to-day they find their most sympathetic expositors
among those with the same background. 'The mutual alienation that
existed between the Baldwin-Chamberlain-Halifax establishment and
the idealistic Left-Wing youth of the universities is something impossible to imagine if you did not experience it,' claims Cyril Connolly.[4]
As one of the idealistic Left-Wing youths of that time, I find this
nonsense. Baldwin, whom I met when he was Chancellor of St. Andrews
University, was prepared to debate with 'youth' and the latter prepared
to listen and argue back. If Philby's own boasts are to be believed,
he was doing under-cover Communist work long before the word
'appeasement' made its appearance in Left-Wing vocabulary. Until
Eden's resignation as Foreign Secretary, Chamberlain was not much of
a hate-focus while Halifax enjoyed a certain Left-Wing sympathy
because of his tolerant attitude towards Indian nationalism and after
Munich was more pitied than hated. And I do not recall either Burgess
or Philby (I hardly knew Maclean) ever recollecting with much

[3] 'I might describe to you the exultations and the rejoicings of James and
his brethren when they heard of the victories of Marengo, Ulm, and Auster-
litz: and how in their little parties of two and three, they walked a mile
farther together in the fields, or by the sides of the Tweed, or peradventure
indulged in an extra pint with one another, though most of them were
temperate men,' writes the author of *Wilson's Tales of the Borders* (published
circa 1840 by James Ainsworth, Manchester). In his story *The Leveller* he
quotes the weaver, James Nicholson, on Napoleon:

'He has been an instrument in humbling the Pope, the instrument
foretold in the Revelation: and he has been the glorious means o' levelling
and destroying the Inquisition—but this sin o' putting away his wife and
pretending to marry another casts a blot upon a' his glories and I fear that
humiliation as a punishment, will follow the foul sin.

'But hae patience a little—the storm will gie place to sunshine, the
troubled waters will subside into a calm and liberty will fling her garment o'
knowledge and mercy owre her now uninstructed worshippers.'
[4] Article in *Sunday Times*, 18.2.68.

concern the major issue which concerned my sort of Left-Wing youth, namely, mass unemployment.

There may have been an element of 'dare' with both Burgess and Philby when they first realized how far they had committed themselves to the Russian intelligence service and had to decide whether to come clean or carry on. But Philby was probably indulging in a post-facto rationalization after years of being a 'double' had given him a sense of estrangement, when he wrote: 'Before one betrays one has got to belong. I never belonged.' It was only from 1944 onwards that I came to know him—although in the end I suppose I 'knew' him as well as most of his colleagues in British service. He leaves rather the memory of someone who was trapped than of being a ruthless trapper. In retrospect his off-duty conversations now seem to add up to an anxious search for justification as he enlarged on the defects of our superior officers and our political *dirigeants*. If they were such a wretched *galère* surely his own role could not be so villainous—such may have been his solace.

The professional skill of espionage is the exploitation of human weakness, and if to that is added the cynical residue of the anti-Fascist idealism of the thirties, Philby seems less of an individual than a lost particle. Each passing year made retraction less possible while long before 1951 he must have known that it was only a matter of time before he, Maclean, Burgess and several others would be identified. Perhaps his views about his superiors were the basis for the arrogant belief that he might just get away with it, while his occupational milieu was that of professional breakers of the Ten Commandments so that he was not greatly hindered by more conventional moral inhibitions. That he had some residual sense of shame at betraying those who trusted and befriended him is indicated by some guarded phrase in his occasional messages from Moscow and he appears to have omitted from his memoirs the names of some of his former colleagues who particularly helped him during his years of family distress. At most one can concede him a certain rueful professional regard which one cannot towards his various associates, if not accomplices, who are still at liberty because the proofs which would satisfy a British law court are now unlikely to be available. Some of them continue to follow quite successful careers.

They doubtless console themselves with the thought that their brand of betrayal was no more heinous than that of their Establishment contemporaries who shared their professions of idealism when all the world was young. After the half-century of political opportunism and cynicism which undermined so many allegiances, they can doubtless dismiss 'Donald', 'Guy', and 'Kim' as incidental small-time affairs. 'There is a gap in me where honour used to be,' said Anouilh's Becket but what society suffers from is a vacuum which loyalty used to fill. And when one considers what has been perpetrated upon the British people over the past fifteen years by both Left and Right Establishments, it is not surprising that the loyal toast causes many a good citizen the same embarrassment as a dirty joke at the wrong place and time.

George Blake comes in a different category not because of his Alexandrine Jewish origins nor his first imaginative years in the Dutch resistance, but because of a marked Walter Mitty streak. When I first noticed this, I had put it down to introspective habits acquired in his North Korean prison camp. Only too late did I realize—as did others —that his Walter Mitty compulsions were his strongest ones. And from his day-dreams, accentuated by the hot-house psychology of prison camp, may have developed the temptation or the challenge— in essence the same urge—to play the great spy in the pay of both Britain and Russia. In one of his dreams, Walter Mitty too was a Master Spy refusing the bandage for his eyes as he faced the firing squad in the grey dawn with a light laugh on his lips.

But betrayal it was to the East Germans who had trusted Blake and who were arrested, tortured, and hanged. And to his British colleagues in a profession which he had freely entered. Not that he had ever been discriminated against because of his origins. On the contrary he was made something of a pet which was a mistake. The British should have perhaps played harder to get! For too internal a life brings too easy an external betrayal. It turns into a twisted form of the power complex. This desire for the secret inner power of knowledge is one which Civil Service Selection Boards increasingly encounter among young candidates and do well to note. It was already recorded some three and a half centuries ago by John Donne:

> He like a priviledg'd spie, whom nothing can
> Discredit, Libells now 'gainst each great man.
> He names a price for every office paid;
> He saith, our warres thrive ill, because delai'd;
> That offices are entail'd, and that there are
> Perpetuities of them, lasting as farre

As the last day; And that great officers,
Doe with the Pirates share, and Dunkirkers.
Who wasts in meat, in clothes, in horse, he notes;
Who loves whores, who boyes, and who goats.[5]

This brings us closer to the basic motivation. Were the spies extreme cases of some necessity in human make-up and common to hero and anti-hero? There is certainly a link between Walter Mitty and our more romantic 'dares'. To the new arrival from more spartan theatres of war, the main fascination of wartime Cairo was not the cream cakes in Groppi's nor the serried ranks of red-tabs in Shepheards, but the dozens—at the time they seemed hundreds—of wistful young officers (and how wistful the English can look when they try hard) with their studied nonchalance, corduroy trousers, and copies of either *The Peloponnesian Wars* or *The Seven Pillars of Wisdom*. Achilles' helm could be sensed if not seen.

And very effective they were in their lone dangerous roles and in standing up to Gestapo torture and partisan treachery. They had their little pleasures from bumping off tribesmen and Balkan peasants who had naïvely misjudged the outcome of Great Power clashes and preferred a quiet life under the SS. to heroics which would ensure M.C.s and D.S.O.s for intrusive British liaison officers. And when it was all over the wistful ones wrote delightful books about each other. I had already encountered a somewhat special breed of the same species. When a truly Imperial force of Gold Coast, Nigerian, and East and South African brigades, with United Kingdom and Indian supporting troops, finally moved over to the assault in 1941 in East Africa, sadness and disapproval were the main reaction of the elderly white-haired second lieutenants of the Kenya Regiment as they recalled the halcyon months of 1940 when they withdrew before the Italians.

'In those days there was only the youth of Kenya,' they remarked as they consumed someone else's slender NAAFI stock and tuned the camp radio to Nairobi to hear the latest report on the Erroll murder trial. 'We were Kenya gentlemen defending our own soil.' The Kenya day-dreams served their purpose in 1940 although they did not help much in 1960 when the late Mr. Iain Macleod's Westminster dreams had precedence over East African realities. But there was also the unhappy face of Wingate in Addis Ababa after his Abyssinian sideshow

[5] Satyres IIII, 1633.

was over and the curtain had been rung down and nobody was interested any more in either his past feats or his neurotic hangover. So to
relieve himself with a new dream and to relieve others of his pestering,
British lives were squandered to no purpose in Burma. And it all seems
one with the tale of the national hero of the previous generation as
T. E. Lawrence is revealed—whatever his courage—as a twisted
masochist unable to tell the truth to superior officer, ally, or
friend.

The tale has of course its comic relief. In 1951 when suffragis and
vendors disappeared from the Suez Canal Zone, there was a delightful
revival of the chumminess of war and the Colonel's wife and Judy
O'Grady met in NAAFI queues to swop their successes in overcoming
hardships, inventing entirely imaginary new ones and describing
how they managed to get hold of some canned concoction. A new
romanticism was built up round baked beans, a new hierarchy of
heroines was created, and shared dreams became common assumptions
for action. And when there are peacetime substitutes such as shortages,
railway breakdowns, and frozen pipes, joy breaks in again and all can
share with gusto their reminiscences.

In the political field, day-dreams can have practical consequences
such as those myths of insularity with their subtopian snobberies and
pretences which the British could carry overseas and pass off as imperialism. Realized as the protocol of the vice-regal court and of countless
government houses, they even acquired a sort of political reality. At
home nowadays it does not take long to establish that the stickit
barristers and journalists and the City hangers-on who make up a
large part of the Tory back benches imagine themselves as country
squires riding up to Westminster to play their part in some ducal
intrigue. Since Professor Oakeshott has proclaimed 'enjoyment in the
thing' as the essence of Tory doctrine, it will take Mr. Edward Heath
some time to get this out of his party: he may not wish to! On the
Labour side the petty Machiavellianism of the expedient, by which
political decisions are evaded, friends deceived, trade-unions elections
rigged, and loyal subordinates let down, develops its own sort of
romanticism. On no account must the image be betrayed whatever
happens to the others. On the factory floor the rank and file are only
too susceptible to suggestions that they are heroes fighting the 'Boss'
although the latter is only a worried little manager struggling with
costing procedures in between escapist dreams of 'a place' in Sussex or
Hampshire. But none of these pretences can last, if only because libidinal

and aggressive impulses will reassert themselves and human reality will change.

This strain of myth-making—in New as well as Old England—is the persistent factor running through Miss Hannah More's shepherds of Salisbury Plain, Uncle Tom and his Cabin, the romantic radicalism of the Countess of Carlisle, the wistful warriors of the Middle East, Macmillan's play-acting, and the affectation of the part of the hard-headed businessman by super-annuated politicians. It is however a new experience for the British to have had for almost two decades the majority of their political and administrative establishment living in a dream world, although for centuries this has been the case with the Arabs and happened to the Germans during the brief interlude of the Thousand-Year Reich. The element of calculation in our make-up closes round the self so that greed takes increasingly short-sighted forms; self-flattery and self-interest are only too easily reconciled and it is the interests of others which we find quite intolerable. In this setting it is hard to sustain traditional loyalties.

We can now begin to sense the nature of that Oriental combination of cunning and greed, pushed to the point of blindness yet coupled with a need for face-saving, to which others are expected to subscribe. Relationships between persons and groups suffer such distortion that we need only wonder that there are not more Macleans, Burgesses, Philbys, and Blakes: for Walter Mitty has excuses for everything. If there are no worthwhile external objects of allegiance, then dis-loyalty will cease to be sensed as such and all the positive vetting techniques of MI5 will be unable to point to the external characteristics of the traitor, if traitor he can be called. If everyone is leading a fantasy life, can there be true human connection? Poor Bee Fell only wanted company in return for the classified platitudes of Gladwyn Jebb.

British political day-dreaming has never been rudely dispelled by the sort of internal dissensions which racked France, Germany, and Italy in the twenties and thirties and reduced the precariously established states of Eastern Europe, whose peoples had presented the classic examples of tribal loyalty in the revolts of 1848, to internecine authoritarian factionalism. Under stress of war and occupation the political fission of French loyalties was polarized even further between Vichy and Gaullisme, collaboration and resistance, and the internal feuds of the *résistants* themselves. While the Communists wrapped themselves in dialectic arguments which gave them the illusion of being prime movers in history and Right-Wing leaders indulged in the flamboyant and phoney-like characters in a Delacroix painting, real resistance was supported by the residual undramatic patriotism of the workers, such as the *cheminots* who in June 1944 moved as one man to back the Allies by action and strike. For as long as one can recall the French people have been better than their leaders.

Even over the two preceding years, as Vichy governors and commanding officers gave themselves up or were captured after gestures of opposition, their famous oath of loyalty to Pétain dissolved in the hair-splitting niceties of the protocol of military surrender, bargaining their order of battle and secret documents in return for the privileges and ration scales appropriate to their prisoner-of-war rank under the Geneva Convention. On those at least they stood firm, for all the world like the *pion* in a French lycée ever watchful lest he was being done out of his daily entitlement of meat, bread, and wine. For, after 180 years, of such are the *droits de l'homme et du citoyen*.

And when it was all over, French intellectuals rapidly renewed the old pre-war solipsistic debate on political commitment, trying to argue out the nightmares of the Nazi occupation in terms of the necessity for suffering and betrayal, laying their own bleeding hearts on the butcher's block for all—particularly francophile British academics and journalists—to admire. The events of 1968 revealed how thin was the crust of national unity apparently restored by De Gaulle's policy of ambiguous rhetoric. In France the discovery of the occasional spy or traitor evokes less concern than in Britain: jealousies over promotion or lack of it are ever and again the prime cause of treason and there is a general assumption that the traitor was betraying somebody else's interest but not one's own. The rotten foundations of 1940 have not yet been repaired.

Under stress and strain of war the Italians behaved very much better than the enemies of Fascism had led us to expect although still adhering to their national operatic tradition. They were either hero or villain, martyr or *traditore*, handing over with appropriate dramatic flourish their swords and their ciphers. Since we were interested in the latter we may unwittingly have offended them by the rather casual way we accepted the former although swords mattered so much to Italian senior officers at those moments when identity depends on dignity. But contrary to expectations, the Allied intelligence services up to the Badoglio armistice of 1943 had little luck in finding highly placed Italian traitors and could only believe with an effort that the king and Fascist Grand Council really planned to depose the Duce.

There was an answer to this riddle. The heavily decorated generals, who proffered while still enemies their order of battle in unasked-for detail and even requested maps to help pinpoint R.A.F. targets on their own headquarters, were matched by junior officers and soldiers who boldly stepped through German minefields at Anzio to guide their new-found Anglo-American allies. For solo performance rather than group solidarity remains the Italian *forte* and the noisy denunciations and accusations which emerged after the Badoglio take-over revealed how hollow had been the structure of a regime whose favourite slogans had emphasised honour, loyalty, and comradeship. The lack of success of Allied intelligence was explained less as a consequence of loyalty than of a certain fastidiousness among the officer caste, aristocracy, and upper bourgeoisie in signing themselves out of any action for or against the Duce.

This could again prove Italy's undoing. The upper class and the better-off sit back and make their elegant jokes about the cliques of lower middle-class politicians who play the musical chairs of office and even resemble physically the burly little men who, in obviously recently unpacked civilian suits, were to be found in the vicinity of Blackshirt militia headquarters during the Allied advance. '*Mai fatto soldato*', they expostulated in spite of being identified as Console-Generale Questo or Quello. So to-day the basic Italian need for some expression of group resentment—of provinces against the centre and of less well-off against the more ostentatious forms of wealth—is met by the Communists. 'These people really aren't Marxists,' claim the fastidious ones. Maybe not. But neither were they Fascists. The quinto-cento moral innocence of the average Italian may preserve his human qualities against ideologies but it does not safeguard his country against takeovers by condottieri, bandits, or commissars. The structure remains hollow.

Neither is restoration of *die deutsche Treue* complete, nor is it at all certain how it will be effected. The initial appeal of Naziism had been to loyalty and seemed for a time to have paid off, so that when collapse came the reversal, the recriminations and back-biting, went to an extreme. But historically *Neid*—envy—has been the overweening German characteristic rather than *Treue*. Hitler knew how to direct envy into anger and defeat intensified it. So the sense of guilt for which the victors so hopefully looked and which Western writers and journalists, particularly those of Jewish origin, are still trying to trace in the German psyche proves elusive. Horror at the past perhaps, but guilt: No!

It could not exist. For in the Weimar Republic there was precious little evocation of personal responsibility and no national focus of loyalty. German society between the wars rested on an uneasy quagmire of fears and resentments. The progressive intellectuals who monopolized Press and social sciences sneered at both the vanished imperial order and the new bourgeois republican respectability. In spite of their Left-Wing views they were at one with the Right-Wing student body of the German universities in their rejection of the Republic: with *Beamtentum, Reichswehr,* and police they shared a preference for élitist notions. And having done their subversive work they fled into exile at the first sign of danger, leaving a confused people with the task of coming to terms with naked power.

So once Goebbels had taken care of everyone's resentments, there was no widely based set of alternative ideas on which resistance to Naziism could have been built. That the generals and others hesitated and lost is not to be wondered at. Only utter dedication to another cause with a focus of loyalty outside Germany could sustain the suicidal effectiveness and self-sacrifice of the group who formed the Russian-controlled 'Red Orchestra'. The Western cause could find no better contact with the growing disillusionment of Germans than the devious Adam von Trott zu Solz with his protestations of being a 'coot Cherman' and the shifty Abwehr agent, Gisevius. At least Germans now seek a new attachment to 'Europe', a new sense of belonging to the community of peoples of the Western seaboard, and that is for us all an important advance. But this search has still to battle against the dominant human factor of envy and the monthly cases of espionage in Bonn reflect the conflict of *Treue* and intrusive *Neid*. Alberich still whispers over Hagen's shoulder in the moment before the dawn.

Before there can be a 'European' loyalty there are many other such spirits of the thirties to be exorcized. In Britain it is always easier to find villains on the Right and heroes on the Left with the corollary that betrayal of one's fellows finds ready justification if it has been for a Left-Wing cause. Our political labels had begun to acquire this illusionary character almost as soon as the Treaty of Versailles was signed in 1919. Churchill was suspect for having helped to promote the intervention in Russia and Reynaud for approving Poincaré's occupation of the Ruhr, so that two of the ablest statesmen of Western democracy suffered eclipse when they had most to offer. Franco and his opponents re-endowed the illusions with an appearance of reality so that for a large section of the Labour Party they are still the only 'reality'. There was a hectic phase just before the outbreak of World War Two when we projected 'Fascist' and 'Anti-Fascist' on to practically every European politician in sight: busy-bodies like Miss Elizabeth Wiskemann dashed round Europe to relabel them for Kingsley Martin's weekly soap opera of goodies versus baddies. Gallant little nations became menaces overnight, the Czech heroes of World War One found they lived in a distant country of which we knew nothing, M. Léon Blum wept copious tears in Downing Street, and one day we woke up to find that Stalin and Hitler had signed a pact and all the time there had been a reality of power of which we had really known nothing.

As soon as the war was over we returned as quickly as possible to the old attitudes. Although it was difficult for even the *New Statesman* to underwrite all Stalin's post-war policies, it found a substitute by lauding the 'Partisan blue' of Jugoslav airmen (the cloth was supplied by the R.A.F. who had in turn taken the colour from the Czarist cavalry tunic) and the 'hammer-like blows of Chinese Communist armies' while at the same time finding plenty of Western uniforms and armed actions to denounce. And since the die-hards were so successful in hanging on to a past image and furbishing it up, a whole post-war generation had willy-nilly to fall in with it. So in the train the faces of *The Times* newspaper readers reflected the rosy vacuous quality of the editorials. Even before one recognized the print one knew that the slightly younger passengers with rather drawn faces, wearing defiant tweeds and the brown brogues of dissent, were busy with the *Guardian*. Up to a year or two before her death, the late Duchess of Atholl still opened the *Daily Worker*, as it still was. But in her case there was a difference: as she read it she became angrier and angrier, finally crushing it in a ball as she disembarked at Sloane Square on her way to some Eastern European refugee work. Poor Red Duchess of the thirties! The images had tarnished for her. But at least she got off at an intermediate stop while *Guardian* readers go on past Westminster, Temple, and the rest, and next morning are still in their Inner Circle, the headlines still reading: U.N. Calls For Action. And that is about as close as most of them will get to action.

So the meaning of treason is not to be found in the flotsam and jetsam of war and espionage, but rather in a complex interplay of the inner man and outward pressure and in a setting where our liege-ideas encourage betrayal. Over the last four decades the process has if anything been intensifying. The preference for one cause rather than another can hardly be labelled as treason if our leaders themselves switch causes whenever it suits them. All a traitor has to do is to persuade himself that he is remaining true to himself. And the formal version of treason is reduced to farce when a patriotic Briton and fighter ace in the shape of Mr. Ian Smith is categorized as fit for incarceration in the Tower of London. This but underlines the fact that loyalty is to be found at its strongest and simplest among those who have experienced the outward pressure of danger when men's need for each other is so overweening that betrayal is unthinkable.

The opposite extreme is escape into some unreal realm of action which can be, as in the case of the late Albert Schweitzer, an actual physical environment, provided it is sufficiently different or far-away from the individual's normal habitat to make him feel that his conduct has been thereby enhanced or acquired some 'universal' attribute. He does himself no harm and some good to others but he may also mislead a larger number as to the significance of his act. Schweitzer performed good acts and doubtless felt that he had done himself some good. He could of course have practised his form of self-realization in the towns of his own Haut-Rhin, which offer sad examples of proletarian debasement, and have left Equatorial Africa to the officials and doctors of the French administration, who did not play Bach on the organ but in practical terms were doing as much for the inhabitants. However, this would have denied to those who followed Schweitzer's example a sense of discovering some higher purpose. Perhaps they did discover one as well as enhancing their view of themselves. But those back in Europe who felt in some vicarious way that their personality had been enhanced by Schweitzer's actions may have only acquired an excuse for behaving in an ignoble way in other fields. This is not to decry idealism but to illustrate that action acquires its political and ethical significance from our own consciousness and not from the nature of the act itself.

And into this trap fell the late Dag Hammarskjoeld—the man who tried to turn a lie into a world order. His published diary notes as well as the revelations of his one-time subordinate, Conor Cruse O'Brien, show how reference to an inner image led him step by step into catastrophe. The Suez crisis of 1956 where all parties accepted face-saving ambiguity to cover withdrawal lured Hammarskjoeld a stage further towards the justification of untruth as the instrument of design. Nasser and Ben-Gurion lost no sleep over the truthfulness or otherwise of his assurances: one needed the protection of the United

Nations Emergency Force to re-equip and retrain his forces for the next round and the other was satisfied to know that for the next ten years Egyptian plans for invasion had been disrupted by the Israeli spoiling attack. But Hammarskjoeld misjudged the Congo. No verbal ambiguities could conceal the intrigues and gun-running of Indians and Egyptians. Hammarskjoeld's attempts to buy them off with increasingly anti-Belgian moves became too blatant. When he could no longer deny knowledge of what his subordinates were up to, he pleaded: 'My office depends on their support.' Under Afro-Asian pressure, he produced one set of instructions for Anglo-American consumption, issued a second to one group of subordinates, and behind their backs verbal intructions to another, a risky course of action in an age of wireless communication and interception. And so lie after lie caught up with Hammarskjoeld who twisted and turned to avoid final confrontation with his own falsehood, and crashed to his death.

Like that other Scandinavian, Vidkun Quisling, who also did a stint of international service—under Nansen, Hammerskjoeld followed some neurotic purpose of his own, the inner dream of a search for a philosophy of life which made it easy for him to commit betrayal as long as his image of self was gratified. Since he shared no purpose with others, he could not see that his acts were betrayal and that truth is not in oneself but exists only as troth to others. It was interesting to find W. H. Auden, the rebel anti-Fascist poet of the thirties, threatening to knock down anyone who suggested that Hammarskjoeld might have acted crookedly.[6] However, Auden now seems to have taken up residence in Austria, a land which is trying to bury the thirties in oblivion: perhaps he is too.

And the lie went on after Hammarskjoeld's death. Those who dreaded that it might be revealed were only too ready to canonize the man and so take their own perjury to his grave. The British politicians and officials who a week or two before had been referring to him as 'that two-faced Swedish something-or-another' thronged Westminster Abbey for the memorial service, while posthumous peace prizes were awarded to the man who had launched deceit, violence, pillage, murder and rape in Katanga. Whatever Africans may have thought of European rule, they had at least found that white men usually told the truth. So the Congolese conclusion was: '*N'jia m'wongo fupi.*' The way of a liar is short!

[6] *Encounter*, November 1961.

D

Hammarskjoeld may be an extreme case of the European dilemma —of internal compulsions which have become so strong that external reality, including other human beings, must be bent or destroyed to give them free rein. His countrymen share it to the full: the pessimistic introspection of Swedish intellectuals, their sense of conflict between instinct and rationality, reflect the problems of a community of men with strong peasant appetites and emotions set too quickly in a welfare frame-work while their Lutheranism has degenerated in one generation from faith to a hangover of conscience. The Russian intelligence services have notably had their greatest successes in Sweden, registering an enviable recruitment of general staff officers, senior officials, and key technicians. So it would seem that a society which makes a cult of formal neutrality and is addicted to maximum moralizing about the conduct of other states of the world, can least of all command loyalty at home.

Must being true to oneself always end in either self-betrayal or in betraying others? Is the only choice that between heroic cliff-hanging or forms of sado-masochism where the spymaster moves in to offer solace? For if he is skilled in his profession he will know how to offer an apparent cure. The great mass of sad little spies and informers are lost souls who at last found self-enhancement by being flattered by somebody's attention and made to feel bigger than they were: as every spy trial reveals, the mercenary motive was secondary and the material rewards pitifully small. Failed priests usually make the most effective agents since they thereby recover some sense of vocation. The saddest thought of all is that they have gained some sense of service and adventure from an act of betrayal.

But if leadership demonstrates cunning rather than loyalty to its followers, can it be otherwise? The English style must have some inspiration for its myth-making, for the perpetual game of amateur theatricals where everyone throws her- or himself into playing a part which will substitute for human relationships. They are not difficult parts to devise, like that played by Captain George Bagley-Guffin at Allied Forces Headquarters Algiers somewhere towards the end of 1943. Trying to combat the longueurs of general staff duties, some wag wrote a letter to another staff section putting at the bottom: Copy to Capt. Bagley-Guffin, Room 321—which was a small empty office. In due course the answer came back with Copy to 321 and as the correspondence extended among other sections, copies showered in on the gallant and non-existent captain. And when the correspondence was up-graded to Top Secret and recipients put on the distribution of other hush-hush matters, Bagley-Guffin went on too. One day he was promoted to major and awarded an O.B.E., and doubtless would have continued his career if the joke hadn't become too good for someone to resist spilling the beans. And if the English appear to welcome war, it is because the parts become convincing, dashing commandos can dress up and really behave like dashing young commandos, and officers' messes are thronged with Bagley-Guffins all talking about the copies of the Top Secret letters they received from each other that day. Yet if there is no external intervention such as the Luftwaffe or a mass desertion of suffragis, the human moment fades and the urge to relapse into an unstyle gets stronger, as if there can be nothing between Buckingham Palace and Notting Hill Gate.

Impossible loyalties should therefore logically produce an unstyle —which is precisely what is happening. Although it would seem impossible for self-centred obsessiveness to create mass solidarity, such is the new phenomenon of anarchism. The most publicized examples such as the ragamuffin cults of the young, whether students or not, may in themselves be little more than cowboy and Indian games and could be rapidly brought to a halt, by those who tolerantly support the participants refusing to pay up any longer. But the raga-muffins are not allowed to be left to themselves. They become news for the gutter press. There is money in it for old-clothes men hawking off unused stock as trendy fashions while vendors of assorted filth and rubbish quickly cash in. Before long the 'revolt' is being written up in *New Society* by Lumpenbrick sociologists as the culture pattern of the future.

At this point the movements become useful disruptive tools for those who have power motives for undermining the confidence of the policy-makers of the Western world. An ideology is gleefully found for the whole affair by the surviving German academics who fled from Weimar after they had helped to bring the house down, and by the assortment of dubious Danubians from pre-war Vienna and Budapest who seem to have established squatters' rights in British and American colleges. While they may get a senile thrill from reliving the romantic futilities of youth, it will not be quite so pleasant for the young who have to grow up in a society which will make tough demands on the individual.

And the new romanticism has nothing of the promise of Rousseau. If 'society' was responsible for his 'crime', his obsession was still that of entering an aristocracy: his concern for liberty required constraint and slid easily over into the proposition that popular sovereignty meant tough law-making by an élite. There is no trace of this in the new revolt. 'The adolescent, preoccupied with establishing his own identity, encounters a society which offers no certainties for him to accept or reject and no models to follow, and so one which increasingly induces in its members a sense of impotence. The drop-out, the drug cult, and the protest movements are all comments upon the situation . . . The purposes and values of society are rejected and the official means of change even in democratic countries are too remote to be seen as relevant.'[7] And their prophet has decreed that there will be no lofty ideal at the end of it all. 'The methodical use of "obscenities" in the political language of the "radicals" is the elemental act of giving a new name to men and things, obliterating the false and hypocritical name which the renamed figures proudly bear in and for the system. And if the renaming invokes the sexual sphere, it falls in line with the great design of the desublimination of culture, which, to the radicals, is a vital aspect of liberation.'[8]

So the new cult of sado-masochism has a preference for espousing lost causes—Guevara, Biafra, Anti-Apartheid, El Fatah. But then why not the Kurds, Eritreans, Yemeni tribesmen, Nilotic peoples of the Sudan, the tribes in Soviet Russia who are being hopelessly and cruelly crushed and even exterminated? The choice seems peculiar until one comes back to the notion of 'our crime'. The crimes of others are irrelevant and as with a character in Dostoevsky it gradually begins to dawn that we must destroy ourselves for this unnameable guilt. Turning Che Guevara into the Horst Wessel of this cult requires something more than the usual literary conceits to cover up the vacuity of the argument. '. . . his envisaged death has become the measure of the parity which can now exist between the self and the world: it is the measure of his total commitment and his total independence . . . he was not submitting to so-called "laws" of history but to the historical nature of his own existence.'[9]

'Existential' thus appears to have degenerated into a vague adjective for any action which has no particular justification. But the great thing

---

[7] Anthony Ryle, *Student Casualties* (Allen Lane: The Penguin Press, 1969).
[8] Herbert Marcuse, *An Essay on Liberation* (Allen Lane: The Penguin Press, 1969).
[9] John Berger, 'The Death of Heroes', *New Society*, 18.1.68.

about the politics of sado-masochism is that they offer the animal get-togetherness of being jointly beaten up by the police and communal indignation afterwards, like old ladies in infirmary waiting-rooms discussing their operational scars. And drop-out anarchism has a literary ancestry of sorts—Huckleberry Finn, Charlie Chaplin, Good Soldier Schweik, and, in his own Prussian way, Leberecht Hühnchen. So there is obviously a career for self-conscious flagellants who can play up to the prevailing mood of indulgence by producing guilt-variant thrills. And for Labour rank and file the whole phenomenon is a godsend since it seems to expatiate their guilt in having failed to realize their concepts of equality, social justice, welfare, and the like. The concepts will not be abandoned, of course: they are the only rags of identity available to Labour, to 'progressives', and to the raggle-taggle ones as well. So they come to stand for their opposites with the result that external reality is even less susceptible to analysis by ideas. When the vocabulary of rationality degenerates into the dogmatic fallacy—that a syllogism can validate false premises—ideas will cease to be the focus of action and loyalty. To the dispersal of power will be added a real anarchy of ideas.

It would have been wrong for us to expect that the mass of ideas and notions inherited by the twentieth-century state from monarchical legitimacy, liberal humanitarianism, syndicalism, and Marxism would remain a valid authority for all time. It is most unlikely that their authority can be revived in terms of existing situations. We may not like the manner in which they are being rejected but the agents of change, whether Puritan ranters, *sans-culottes* or *pétroleuses*, are never very attractive. And if we are entering a period of indulgence in strange self-images, in individual inversion, this has in history sometimes been the prelude to an outward burst which after due struggle brings new manifestations of power and allegiance. The Reformation coincided with—if indeed it was not mainly caused by—a need for inward transformation of the individual. It led to a broad popular challenge to the duty of unconditional obedience to princes, particularly in Scotland, France, and Hungary: Knox laid down explicitly that subjects had a duty to rebel against their rulers given sufficient cause. Two hundred and fifty years later, the heightened self-consciousness that began with Rousseau and the *Sturm und Drang* released a century of revolution.

It could go the other way. The present inversion might result in forms of adult autism, of mental development arrested by inability to communicate or act except in utterly trivial terms. 'Causes' would degenerate into incommunicable paranoia so that in the end all one's fellows would become dispensable. If the human need for togetherness cannot be directed overtly and thinkingly or tacitly and intuitively on to some person, idea or institution, it will be perverted to destructive ends. After Weimar Germany we should not discount the risks of any myth-making, even the infantilism of the New Left, breaking out into the furies of inversion. Old quarrels can serve new ends as happened in Ulster, while Canada which two decades ago seemed to have lapsed into a faceless land, suddenly found that it had to stand up and be counted. The mass racial intrusion forced upon the British peoples has created a broad stratum of smouldering resentment which has even been fanned by the blatant sponsorship of the intruders by both Old and New Left. Britain may be at a point of balance which can be tipped either way. The history of the peoples and civilizations of the earth is as much one of regression as of progress. Failure has been more frequent than success in government and more politicians have sunk without a trace than have risen to statesmanship.

The immediate political and social future will not be a very comfortable one for the British. It will probably take longer than one term of Parliamentary office to restore the sense of public order which was weakened under Labour, whose economic, fiscal and racial interventions were directed against those who in most cases obey the laws and rules: it failed completely over those who chose to break them. The unofficial workers' leaders and shop-floor demagogues can still demonstrate that in terms of wage packets, their militancy pays off and inflation can be pushed on to the old, the feeble, and the unmilitant. Jones, Scanlon, and Jenkins, like the French democratic politician of 1848, will continue to cry: 'I am their leader. I must follow them.' Mr. Harold Wilson obviously intends to follow as leader of the Opposition the same style he did as Prime Minister. Loyalty will not characterize the Labour Party.

Yet since ideas too are woven into our self-consciousness and are part of our vocabulary of identity, the recovery of loyalty must involve the rebuilding of a bridge between ideas and action. Withdrawal into Bagley-Guffinesque myth-making on one side and indulgence in self-conscious guilt imagery on the other will not achieve this, nor will attachment to the liberal-humanitarian-egalitarian ideas which are now being invoked destructively. But must we be forever attached to such ideas? Can Britain have no identity without them? British laws and their constitutional embodiments antedated by more than two centuries universal suffrage, broad-based Parliamentary representation, and social egalitarianism. Our national ways, although they do not fit into the intellectual categories of the emigré professors and sociologists from Weissnichtwo, are not just to be dismissed as 'historicism'.

If at any time in any society the situation—to adapt the old Austrian quip—though desperate is never hopeless, this is because of the foundation of trusting people, those who must trust or they will die. Their daily necessities form the basis of human co-operation which *is* society —the farmer who must sow and reap, the ploughman who seeks work, the smith who has metal to forge, the chemist with a process, and the banker who provides the media of trustful exchange. They can cope with many ideas. In our lifetime we have seen this dramatically. As the Allied armies entered Germany in the spring of 1945 it seemed as if Europe's days were over. Towns were flattened deserts of rubble and famous international concerns tangled masses of scrap-iron. Along the verge of every main highway straggled two apparently unending columns of ragged and hungry human beings, one mainly Slav heading east, the other—Dutch, Belgians, and French—coming west. And from time to time one passed great stockades of surrendered men in shabby grey uniforms.

Could Europe ever rise again? It did. Not because anyone produced a new startling concept nor because a professor had a theory, but simply because men and women picked up the strands of daily life and wove them back into human societies. They eventually reached a point where as individuals they could do little more and sought as guide some valid collective concept. But under the surface phenomena of catastrophe, there remained the unbroken continuity of human needs and the skills to meet them and neither needs nor skills are contingent things of yesterday. They are the determining and limiting elements which with each dawn suggest not necessarily that the day will be the same as the one before, but that it will unroll within a known range of possibilities and even probabilities.

This human foundation is always taken for granted. Looking at the social structure of north-western Europe, Caesar noted in *De Bello Gallico*: 'The common people are regarded almost as slaves. They possess no initiative and their views are never invited on any question.' Yet it was they who restored the first tenuous threads of the European fabric at a time when its prospects of survival were at their dimmest. The first peasants and craftsmen who ventured into the Viking camps of the Seine Estuary and of the English Danelaw to peddle goods and skills established the first rapport between invaders and invaded. 'Only peasants rubbing shoulders with peasants would have been able to teach their neighbours new names for bread, egg, or root. . . . In their languages too was an analogous order of ideas.'[10] And some Viking hearts were touched. The Icelandic sagas tell of a raider who was nick-named 'the children's man' because he refused to follow his companions' custom of impaling them on the point of his spear.

And after one generation the Norse raiders had established themselves as one of the ablest governing classes of history. They had turned Roman concepts of rule and law to new practical use, enlisted Christian clerics as their civil servants, and created a new form of allegiance among peasants and townsmen. Even at the Byzantine court only the Norse guards could be entrusted with the protection of those born in the purple. And from the intermingling of the skills and ideas of the 'Dark Ages'—the improved ploughshares, grinding mills, stock breeding, and new arts of war and fortification—came the new European thrust which drove Arab and Magyar raiders back to their own lands and carried the Europeans even beyond the seas. No similar abiding link was created between European peasantry and the Saracen camps of Provence and northern Spain; at most the Sephardic Jew flitted back and forward with his wares and the Arabs retreated to their epigonic Byzantine culture of temples-turned-mosques, steam baths and cribbed Hellenistic manuscripts. The massive slave raids of the Magyars had at least provided priests, teachers, and craftsmen from the West so that it is to the West that Hungary belongs to-day.

When the human qualities of strength and trust combine in a fresh setting of ideas, not only survival but advance and expansion are the consequence. And since the process of Europe has been a continuous one it should be able to reveal to us the nature of our malady to-day and perhaps even the remedy, so that tomorrow we can resume the advance with a new allegiance. It will not be a comfortable task such as a Gallo-Roman villa owner might ponder as he mulled over the thoughts of Epicurus. There is no faith as in the seventh and eighth centuries which the monks could carry along with their manuscripts, crop seeds, and vine-cuttings, to be nurtured afresh in some land far from

[10] Marc Bloch, *Feudal Society* (Routledge & Kegan Paul, 1961), pp. 44–5.

Saracen and Magyar. We seem to be in a worse state than the Germans under Naziism which aimed at destroying others, while we are asked to make a virtue of self-destruction. It is not the named traitors we have to fear but a betrayal through ideas.

III. Young Werther Lives!

III. Young Werther Lives!

One special factor was at work in the European process which has been absent in other eras and in other areas of conquest. Descriptions and explanations became new sets of ideas exchangeable between conquerors and conquered and have formed the basis for new methods of rule and new institutions of authority and community. Here seems to be the genotype—the type that creates. Neither the inheritance of Rome by itself nor the spread of Christianity can explain this or the same phenomenon would have been evident among the inhabitants of the Levant and of North Africa. And all the peoples of the former Roman and Byzantine Empires shared the same basic needs of human societies anywhere—physical security, the assurance of some order where groups and individuals could lead their lives with a minimum of arbitrary molestation, some notions of law and religion which would be respected as more or less binding by law-givers and subjects.

Such general notions are to be found over the whole earth in any culture worth the name. And as far as first-order factors of human consciousness are concerned, in all races of mankind the individual sense of identity has been born from the awareness of a separation between himself and what is external to him, between subject and object. It will be found in Bushman and in Bostonian. But the peculiarly European second-order factor is that the individual has increasingly endeavoured to confirm this identity in terms of objective creations or what he can assume to be such.

Outside the Western European peoples and their overseas projections, there has for better or for worse been no similar steady growth of conscious individuality determined by this interplay of subjectivity and objectivity and reassessed in the form of new conscious concepts. Even if older tribal bonds still persisted and from time to time revived as during the migrations and turmoil of the Dark Ages, European authority and loyalties, except under severe external pressures, could never again be purely instinctive. By the twelfth century, conceptual reconstruction had been extended to what we believed to be our knowledge of self, so that after an interruption of some centuries the speculative process which had begun with the Greeks was again in full swing. And at each stage of the process new frontiers of identity were drawn so that by the fourteenth century the 'open' Europe of the twelfth was no more.

The first causes of this special relationship between Europeans and their objects of consciousness can never be known to us except through hypothetical reconstruction. Its biological basis may well be the cycle of advance and retardation in childhood, puberty, and adolescence found among peoples of mainly Caucasoid descent. And although the nomadic-pastoral life with its varying cycles of migration and settlement was not uniquely European, it is one of the rarer primitive socio-economic patterns and does heighten the dichotomy between a need for order and permanence and the urge to free oneself of encumbrance. Linguistic change has played its part. Few of the peoples of Western Europe, centre of the efflorescence, speak the languages which were native to them over the tens of thousands of years when they were groping through the instinctual and emotional world of pre-history. A gap between emotions and utterance contributes an element of tension which can add to intellectual potential, just as the proto-human effort in switching from one animal skill to another created the human potential for self-consciousness.

Linguistic change may also be world-wide but the European languages were cognate enough to be readily grasped and exchanged and during the periods of linguistic change there was sufficient mutual interaction for imagination to cross and recross the gaps with fresh usage. Language has thus in Europe become something more than emphatic or indicative communication: it early became a framework for conveying sets of ideas. The linguistic factor which on one side created distance between subject and object, could also suggest metaphors for reuniting them and is still at work among us. Borrowing and lending of tongues creates a tradition of communication without emotional commitment and if it can cool human relations and thus heighten our inner loneliness, it can also contribute an additional instrument of mental conquest.

As if this were not enough, Europeans had also to borrow a religion from outside when older myths had ceased to satisfy as explanations for external nature and for the uncertainties of human destiny. And having settled for Christian imagery as the most sympathetic of the available Oriental cults, one which offered consolation when all around was turmoil and cruelty, we set about trying to endow it with an intellectual coherence no religion could ever possess. By the twelfth century too, the Catholic faith—so called for the first time—had to be presented as a discipline to be taught and learned, so that what had offered emotional release and objects of reverence became a restraint of the will. One of the first great creations of European rationality thus rested on contradictory premises. The dichotomy was sharpened: heresy and revolt were the immediate reaction and have gone on since.

The conclusion is that Europeans cannot be restrained from trying to make conceptual reconstructions of their own past and have generally expressed them in the form of intellectual contrasts. The process has been going on since earliest recorded European history and successive reconstructions have resulted in the institutionalizing of both customary growths and conscious inventions so that we have long since lost sight of the delimitations between human qualities and created objects. Each generation displays ever greater determination to ascribe objective and universal value to inherited institutions, even if their origins were in habits, traditions, or subjective feelings of group identity and their apparent legitimacy derived from purely local coincidence. At times human loyalties and institutional allegiances became very uneasy bedfellows: the most unlikely practices were idealized as the path of virtue, as for example the sordid intrigues of the 'Glorious Revolution' institutionalized as the management of Parliament. The mercenary factions of Whig and Tory were confirmed as a Parliamentary party system which we blandly assumed to be best for all mankind. The first exportation of this system to our neighbour France, bound to us by common events of history and so akin to us in spheres of the intellect, failed completely: her four Republics were undermined by faction and fear of faction. But in this year of grace we are still insisting that it should be imposed on non-Europeans to whom the system is utterly alien.

Not all men in Europe shared in the process in equal measure or within the same time scale. Europe's geography of peninsulas and river valleys, its human variety, material divisions and conflicts ensured that the process would be slow and uneven. The peasantry continued a largely instinctive life coloured by the animism inherited from the days when all the world was one. Up to the fourteenth century the nomadic instinct competed with the satisfaction of settlement. Those who by nature preferred action to speculation found abundant opportunity for the release of physical energy and needed no objective explanations for their actions. The sword, as well as thought, could reach the bounds of the known universe. This basically physical urge still colours our mental world with strange analogies about 'outward looking'.

But as a sense of identity developed, the need for permanence grew stronger and the aspect of the European historical process which becomes most marked is our passionate attachment to the objects of our own creation. Since these have become the authority on which the sense of identity depended, to release hold on them would have thrown men back into insecurity. The European rejection of trial by combat and retributive justice reflected the need for laws which would protect men against arbitrariness or at least identify an arbitrary act as such. And when arbitrary or ineffective rulers were dethroned, the action had always to be justified afterwards by a reasoned restatement of authority with a preamble setting out the sanction of divinity and of sovereignty. Kings and councils claimed to subscribe to the laws even when they violated them and in our century it was still enough for Kaiser Franz-Josef to write on the margin of a minute dealing with the complaint of a subject: 'Der Minister soll nach dem Gesetz handeln' and start off a Cabinet crisis. Our belief to-day that human progress reflects the advance of reason rests largely on the ever-growing archives of documents set out in reasonable terms and not on the realities of human motivation.

As we delve deeper into the archives, the motives behind the rhetoric and verbal adornment of chanceries and prelates become clearer. The imposition of a legal framework and the apparent intro-duction of a higher principle could be a façade for the lowest calculation of self-interest, as with the papal jurists who under Canon Law legiti-mized 'external crusades' against Slavs and Wends and German peasants. Arbitrary oppression and treachery remain such even if designated *crux cismarina* or *commutatio*. We are not unfamiliar with the process in our own time. The Fourteenth Amendment of the United States Constitution, on which the Supreme Court based its 1960 desegregation decision and as a result of which President Eisenhower ordered his paratroops to Little Rock, was inserted in 1868 by carpet-bagging methods on which the Court itself to this day has never dared to pass an opinion. Yet those who protested against court orders based on this Amendment were denounced as defying the Constitution.

In contrast to this conception, even the most advanced systems of law of non-European peoples derive only from the wisdom or virtues of the rulers. Under Koranic law the cadi must be guided by his sense of the wisdom of Allah or by his valuation of the customary gifts of the litigants, in coming to a judgement. Although most Arab states have introduced codes of European civil law to meet the complexities of modern commercial life, the learned doctors of Al Hazar do not concede to these any objective existence outside the mind of Allah.

Since over the larger part of Europe a formal status as 'man' or as citizen enshrined in statute and secured by orderly administration was a more pressing issue for the individual than political self-expression, emperors and kings survived up to 1918. Where and how a clash of privilege and rights developed may have depended on contingent circumstances such as the skill of a ruler or the sense of responsibility of new privilege seekers. Authority and freedom could often be invoked by either side. Under rulers who concentrated on relations with other rulers and left their subjects free to devise group relationships to their own liking, public restraint was rarely sensed as an abuse of authority. Where rulers were of different race or language, a new emotional factor was liable to emerge as self-consciousness grew.

So here has been no great battle of authority against freedom, no tribal tradition against law. There has been a great deal of human calculation and cruelty, licence, and abuse of privilege by every faction and, in spite of it all, increasing security in daily life. Yet in the time span of European history there has been something more than a disguised clash of material interests. It is now Western men's destiny that they conceive their identity in terms of created objects—words and institutions—rather than through their instincts. The latter still remain, however, playing their part in shaping our consciousness and in determining the quality of our lives.

The discrepancies and the conflicts between ideas and instinct, between the material concerns of rulers and subjects and their common need for a secure identity, could be reconciled after a fashion so long as human energies found ready outlets. So long as Europeans could find freedom for themselves in sallying outwards and imposing *their* authority on others, the uncertain dichotomy of power and emancipation was rarely a critical factor. But the moment one single element in the situation began to assume an overweening importance, the conflicts became less easy to resolve. The disruptive factor proved to be heightened self-consciousness. The greater security and easement of life, particularly among the bourgeois, permitted a new luxury of inward sentimentality leading at times to an obsessive concern with

E

self. The development of humanistic thought since Renaissance and Reformation, and the tendency to tie up religious faith into neat little packets for official and Sunday use, meant that for six days of the week the nature of 'Man' could be the subject of study and the measure of philosophic systems. This at least brought an end to *auto da fé*, to putting Catholic priests on the rack, and tying children who refused to accept the Anglican Book of Common Prayer to stakes in the Solway tide. But it started off a new conflict sensed as one between human expectation and the trammels of society.

Guaranteed civic privilege was not enough for the Romantics. For the super-sensitive the command of the instincts had to be obeyed. Claiming his freedom in everything, the individual was also laying claim to universality popularized in Turgot's thesis of the historical individuality of every man as the substance from which the whole of humanity was built. And all this was backed by the belief of the Enlightenment that cumulative and irreversible knowledge would sanctify the condition of humanity and endow the individual with moral authority and responsibility for choice and decision not only over himself but over others.

In such a setting the concept of 'Man' presaged not only Romantic heroes grappling with obscure inner destinies, but also revolution and new forms of tyranny. The problem faced by poets in past centuries had become that of Europe at large. Although the philosophic and political vocabulary remained that of Reason, the motive power was feeling. The terror of the French Revolution was the handiwork of men brought up under eighteenth-century rationalism and if political Romanticism fastened on any country, it was certainly nineteenth-century France. The republican leaders, the neo-Jacobin pamphleteers and Catholic obscurantists were equally ready to call out the confused rootless proletariat of the shanty-town faubourgs in the name of the mystical Revolution and of the morally regenerative qualities of chauvinism and violence.

A century later one of the curious aspects of Naziism was the ease with which German intellectuals could justify it: its origins may have been in irrational fears and resentments but it could still be formulated conceptually so that the German people attached themselves to it with such adhesive force that they were prepared to march all Europe into destruction. But once an object has engaged our consciousness it can submerge any sense of history or of past experience and in a process where reasoning and feeling are interwoven, the objects may impel us on strange courses which can only be left to run to their end. It is not otherwise with Marxism, particularly in its latter-day fantasy versions.

The consequences of the new intellectual and sentimental convergence round the notion of 'Man' were no more foreseen than those of most European movements. The classical Greeks, to whose direct line of descent the writers of the Enlightenment claimed to belong as they dallied with the fashionable Anacreontic medallions, had handled the concept of Man moderately enough. It had served as the basic concept in mediæval and Renaissance 'Natural Law' while the American rebels had kept it under control in their new Constitution. But where so many human attributes intruded, the assertion of individual identity as 'Universal Man' was a hazardous affair. First symptoms were not long in appearing as numerous young men dressed themselves in blue tail coats and yellow top boots and after writing letters of farewell blew their brains out. Being interesting was at least a substitute for universality, much as hysterical teenagers reach for their barbiturate pills when they read of the suicide of a pop star. But one Corsican officer stayed alive, slept with his copy of Werther under the pillow, and started out to see how universal he could be. He proved to be the first of many.

The development percolated only slowly through the consciousness of Europeans. While old instinctive ways and loyalties continued for many, the new self-conscious Romanticism regarded this as proof of the universal innocence of Man although there is nothing very innocent about a peasant particularly on market day. But there were less happy political consequences. It was no longer enough for a Czech *sektionschef* in the Trentino or an Italian *consigliero ministeriale* in the Bukovina to be helpful and administer the law. He had become an image which clashed with the image of those over whom he was in authority. The pietistic Bohemians and Moravians, after having lived not unhappily for two hundred years under the baroque catholicism and orderly administration of Austria, began to be conscious of their own separate identities. And in Vienna the *herrschaften* were sitting around with extremely self-conscious images waiting for someone to invent psychoanalysis.

Such a situation indicated an impending disintegration with or without explosives. The old allegiances were weakening and it was on an unstable basis that the new patriotism tried to build the national sovereign state. And power too was proving a potentially unstable

element: for while its exercise still required the same sort of temperament and skills for using other men as instruments in a design, its
practitioners had to call on greater arts of dissimulation. So the European process of conceptual reconstruction, with its tendency to encourage mental division, created such a separation of motivation
and rationalization that the demands on self have become greater
than it can bear. This could affect our minds in a fashion which would
reverse the direction of European civilization.

For if human consciousness is self-consciousness, its heightening
can no more be reversed than evolution itself. In theory a stage could
be reached where our consciousness of self would so dominate all
other considerations as to cause complete inversion of the mind. Any
attempt to return to Enlightenment or to any other pre-Romantic
mode of thought becomes itself a Romantic illusion, since conceptual
reconstruction as the very essence of the European mind prevents
any return: there can never be standing still. Our identity has to be
maintained by change! The original object can never be recovered,
the subject can never be disentangled from any of its previous identities.
And if we are all to some degree speaking the language of inversion,
any fresh attempt at conceptualization may bring us up against an
apparently impenetrable mental barrier.

The mental impasse which Europe had reached in its use of humanist concepts had been concealed by the accelerated outward expansion
of empire, settlement, commerce and science over the last century.
But human purpose was no longer the continuation of a mainly
intuitive outward thrust, an essentially naïve relationship between
consciousness and its objects. The subject was not now reaching out
for an object but mulling over the subjective notion of an object and
what he tried to convey to others was less his reaction to it than an
idea about himself in terms of this reaction. In this situation we find
ourselves continually pushing our self-consciousness against an en-
circling barbed-wire fence of concepts originally intended to provide
a rational explanation of the external universe but now a trap for
subjectivity. Only images of self come bouncing back or else hang
lacerated on the wire: small minds seek refuge in the form of barbed-
wire-itis known as positivism and content themselves with asking:
What do I mean when I say?

'Reason' has thus taken strange forms since Kant. Each new
universal version proves on closer examination to be yet another
image of the philosopher's own mind, a tautology for his starting

point, another begging of the question, a justification of his state of mind for being the State. We need not blame the Germans for being the instigators: they had only tried to find an *endlösung* for what our Dr. Johnson had noticed a century earlier to be the professional malady: 'The philosopher rode up and departed with the air of a man that had co-operated with the present system.' Nietzsche rightly sensed that it was a problem for poetry.

Under the circumstances how could the European nineteenth century have been anything but a time of war, revolution, and of academic and artistic conflict? So many minds at different stages of sensitivity and awareness were involved in the process of inversion. So many inherited conceptions had also to be reconciled with external reality. Local factors made the pace still more uneven while group images confronted one another with widely different social, national, and other communal frameworks.

However, 'freedom' did offer some peoples of Europe the prospect of throwing off visible restraint and removing the vested privileges of alien authority: the emotional release thus provided seemed more important than the risk to historically acquired civic rights. Hapsburg and Romanoff subjects set off with plenty of West European liberal encouragement on the path which they believed would lead them to an assured identity and has landed most of them behind the Iron Curtain. The Italians' quest for their own image had some unhappy interludes as they hesitated between the claims of self-centred greed and the sentimental projection of themselves on to flamboyant adventurers. Because they retain in large measure a naïve relationship with persons and objects in which feeling and expression of feeling are indistinguishable, the Italians have suffered less emotional hurt than other European peoples. Whatever the superficies of Italian political forms, their political leaders and spiritual shepherds managed to renew the perennial conspiracy which perpetuates a nice *arrangemento* between material corruption and emotional innocence.

But in Europe as a whole authority did not come off at all well. Those who embodied it were alien, papal, reluctant to give up their own privileges, and had sometimes to use force to protect them (as did the democrats to win theirs), kept mistresses (so did the democratic leaders but not apparently from public funds) and were generally identity-denying. In any case the poets were against them. Even kings who happened to be poets themselves and had romantic ideas about kingship—such as Napoleon III's vision of himself as the standard bearer of progress, or Ludwig II of Bavaria with his passion for fairy castles—found that their dreams sooner or later became irreconcilable with those of their subjects. For the whole mental process involved the transfer of emotion to the object of emotion. Freedom, like all ideas never to be perfectly realized, was easily suffused with sentiments of love for evermore while authority being tangible as a person or group of persons could be fairly seized with hate. There seemed to be no need to worry about the possibility that one day men might again need visible authority and that freedom might no longer offer hopes of identity and certainty.

So while often professing to reject the Hegelian metaphysics of the mind in conflict, Europeans succumbed to the notion of conflict in one form or another and have had to describe the search for a new mix of authority and freedom as a 'struggle'. Malthus put the conflict notion in a natural framework, Bentham in terms of pleasure versus pain, Mill as between justice and freedom. The actual phraseology seems to be contingent on little more than linguistic tradition. So the potential for Mr. Heath's civil wars exists in any society ruled by ideas: for the idea will evoke its opposite and when a concept takes command it will create its own rebel challenger.

And once in office politicians had to seek out a new principle for legitimizing obedience and soon found themselves associated in popular consciousness with the persistence of old privilege, while those in opposition who were still in search of new privilege were reluctant or unable to face the implications of ensuring obedience. Liberal thought solved the issue by dodging it. Academic speculation on the subject came to little more than generalized verbal equations which did nothing to clarify the mental confusion of those dealing with practical issues. In the subsequent conflicts of ideology, the concepts became interchangeable and meaningless—dirty words in somebody's vocabulary, noble ideals in another's. If the consequences have not been worse, it is because of the solid element of material calculation in every cause, the residue of naïve human relationship which ensures social stability, and plain human inconsistency. 'Whatever happens, we must not give up our ideals', we chorus as we release the bombs.

Still! The easement of life and the growth of sentimentality brought greater compassion and the sensitivity of one individual prompted him to reflect on the sufferings of another. Slavery went and so did child labour, while public torture and execution which had been normal spectacles for the men of the Enlightenment were now felt as an affront to 'human dignity', as the bourgeois could now describe his sense of the fitting. It was better that the needful tasks were performed in the prison yard behind closed gates in front of which only the morbid need gather. The naïvely brutal were thereby denied a treat but it was felt that good works and education would eventually awaken in their hearts the same sentiments of humanity. And to a great extent so they did, and it is an absolute gain if greater numbers of enlightened persons, having escaped from the physically and mentally brutalizing influences of material degradation, come forward to play a more active part in the running of society.

But the sentimental self-images can be projected on to the wrong screen. The moral nerve of England is liable to be triggered off by the most unlikely causes. Where these affected the quality of life of our own community—such as the emancipation of slaves, criminal law reform, and social legislation—the reaction was understandable. But the inhabitants of far lands found themselves cast most unaccountably in the roles of hero or villain. And when English self-imagery changed for reasons only vaguely grasped by the English themselves, the heroes and villains found that equally unaccountably their roles had been switched although they had only gone on behaving as Greeks, Turks, Boers, and Arabs always had. Currently our oldest ally, Portugal, which for two hundred years has consistently pursued the same overseas policies, finds itself put in the role of one of the principal villains: and so do the white Rhodesians who continue in practice to administer African affairs as we did ourselves in Crown colonies with much self-congratulatory talk about our duties and our responsibilities. The moral nerve tendons are obviously getting mixed when we confuse 'evil' and inexpedient. If we keep recasting Americans almost monthly from sheriff to outlaw and back again, here there is at least a rough justice since the Americans are just as prone to do the same to their allies. Under such circumstances there is something monstrous about 'Man'. As a notion it has reached a grotesque end-form.

However, since the process was one of the imagination, the arts were the first to gain. By giving us a communicable vision of the object and not merely its reproduction, the true artist of whatever age and style can stimulate our strongest intuitions of permanence. When we project our self-consciousness back on to the visionary creations of past ages, they seem to speak to us in terms of our own emotional predicaments. By the beginning of the nineteenth century the outward symptoms of the new stage reached were the need to make a vision convincing in contemporary terms, the disappearance of anachronism except as a self-conscious mannerism, and the new fashion for local colour. Hamlet and Macbeth could no longer be played, as in Zoffany portraits, looking like Hogarthian rakes worried about the pox. Alfred de Vigny's Lord Mayor enters Chatterton's garret from the wings 'gonflé de rostbif et de porter'. Since subjectivity shifts not only with each generation but now within a generation, this becomes an accelerating process in the arts. To-day's emotional intensity which we like to describe as the truth of our emotions becomes tomorrow's sentimental conceit, and yesterday's visions acquire the insipidity of Landseer's anthropomorphic stags and hounds or of *Bubbles* and *The Last Night in the Old Home*.

It is in the novel that our subjective images of self are most easily reconciled with the artist's evocation. And the shift of novel and drama from the picaresque and flamboyant to the introspective and agonized not only highlights what had been happening but pointed to the future. The nineteenth-century hero, unlike the politician, was under no compulsion to lie to himself. So Young Werther can dress by the right with Lucien Leeuwen and join Tolstoy's young officers searching on the battlefield for the significance of life, and finish up with our own heroes of conscience rebelling against they know not what.

And when the major problem of our time has become one of imagination with elements of subconscious and fully conscious play-acting, the novel begins to provide some explanations even for the mysteries of Cabinet decisions. For our Ministers play at being, if not Disraeli, at least characters from his novels, our generals discourse on Bellerophon, and the run-down of political ideas is reflected in the cult of the failed image. 'I might still take Holy Orders when I retire . . . At heart I'm a publisher . . . Bird watching is really my main interest.' A harmless enough conceit, so one might say, until we recall the failed artist of Linz who eventually got the German masses as a subject for artistic recreation and then we look at our own masses whose imagination has been touched just sufficiently to sense that they too are starved of objects they can honour and revere.

For a potent factor which the introspective process has brought into being is a new growth of affective communication which differs in essentials from old naïve forms, including those which preceded even verbal communication. Joy, hate, anger, fear, affection and suspicion are all communicated by association not by argument, and issues can now be so cunningly misrepresented that a man can be made to fear himself for nourishing dangerous thoughts and can discover in himself a *Schweinhund* planted by others. Multi-meaning concepts can be used unscrupulously to evoke a multitude of images and mislead men as to where their common interest lies. British eighteenth-century politics provided classic examples of personal abuse and name-calling but contemporary fraudulent associations of ideas create a different quality of illusion.

Such techniques can fire a people with a sense of mission but no one can guarantee what in the final outcome will be the type of image the participants will try to realize for themselves, and what form of release the doubts and frustrations hitherto hampering their desire for self-expression will take. The chords struck in men's hearts may find a response not intended by the player so that human communication itself may be completely changed in quality. On one hand the images may increase the individual's mental isolation, on the other there may be unexpected and terrifying forms of group contagion. Myths and illusions can of course be beneficent: the pastoral-cum-chivalresque myths of the early mediæval romances based on older legends are said to have developed into the codes of honour of courts and chivalry, and eventually became the catechisms of bourgeois honesty and obligation. But myths can also burn witches. 'Controlled' myths playing their part in the instruction of rising confident élites are one thing. When let loose upon masses who have ceased to have a sense of individual identity, they can have other consequences.

For this is where Turgot and Young Werther have brought us. The concept of the historical individuality of every man has crossed its finishing line with the loss of confidence in ourselves as individuals. In ceasing to create new political and social concepts based on genuine human experience and by hanging on to irrelevant notions, we expose ourselves to the impact of a series of substitute images of ourselves which in so far as they relate to human attributes are likely to operate destructively. The image of Man has been taken over by projectionists whose aims and methods are in direct contradiction to the professed ideals of society.

We can just about cope with the traditional political projectionists since we knew their forbears in our naïver days. But the commercial image-makers, who merit a certain respect for being the first to spot what was happening to our minds, have devised more subtle techniques. We are exhorted to identify ourselves with some object which we shall never dare let go—be it soap, deodorant, underwear, or something out of a bottle. And since the system can only flourish by perpetuating our sense of inner security, we must at all costs be prevented from reacquiring a sense of security and be given fresh jolts of fear. We have worried lest human deterioration could set in through civilization being materially destroyed. We had hardly expected it to come about through too rapid material advance. The mass of new inventions, instead of stimulating men with zest for new ventures, is being mis-applied to try to ensure that each day they wake up with a new load of imagery created expressly to deny them individual experience. In this state the mind either shrinks or becomes neurotic.

The crime here is that the target is just that sceptical yet loyal mass who have provided stability when ideas have been unstable, solidarity when disintegration threatened, and courage when surrender was in the air. The most profitable and effective appeal is obviously to the lowest common denominator and so far there is no indication that we have reached bottom. The 'dope' does not in fact stifle neurosis. It stimulates it and adds to the growing violence of society. Mr. Arthur Koestler desperately produces a plan for a universal dope to save the human race from destruction.[1] The Sage of Ecclefechan had already snorted that solution out of existence: 'Resolutely once gulp down your Religion, your Morrison's Pill, you have it all plain sailing now: you can follow your affairs, your no-affairs, go along money hunting, pleasure hunting, dilettanting, dangling, and miming and chattering like a Dead Sea Ape: your Morrison will do your business for you. Men's notions are very strange. Brother, I say there is not, was not, nor will ever be, in the wide circle of Nature, any Pill or Religion of that character.'[2]

But sadly enough, British politics for twenty-five years have been increasingly conducted in the belief that it pays to keep Caliban down. Bagehot's summing-up of Palmerston could apply equally to Macmillan. 'He a little degraded us by preaching a doctrine just below our own standard: a doctrine not enough below us to repel us much but yet enough below to harm us by augmenting a worldliness which needed no addition.'[3] The consequences of Macmillan are more serious since up to the end of the nineteenth century there was still

---

[1] *The Ghost In The Machine* (Hutchinson, 1967).
[2] *Past and Present*, Book III, Chapter XV.
[3] *The English Constitution* (O.U.P., The World's Classics, 1966), p. 151.

some trust, even if mixed with scepticism, between British politicians and their followers. After the 1959 election victory, one or two other Tory leaders, particularly Mr. Reginald Maudling, began to mutter of the unwisdom of moral self-flattery coupled with material appeals. But in both State papers and in smoking-room conversations, Macmillan appears to have succumbed to the satisfying notion that he was Bagehot's statesman 'in quiet times' and priority should be given to 'not raising questions which would excite the lower orders of mankind'. The outcome was a failure to set the fresh policy aims which the changing relationship between the United States and Europe required, the drift into a quite unnecessary economic tangle from which Britain has not yet got clear, and the saddling of the British working class with two million coloured slum dwellers.

However, by 1960 the majority of Macmillan's Cabinet colleagues had joined in this self-conscious posturing. The least tasteful was the late Mr. Iain Macleod's image of himself as a shrewd and skilful player of men as well as of cards, emerging triumphantly from his first Lancaster House conference as Colonial Secretary telling all and sundry how his smart phrases had solved the problem of his own position in his party, bluffed his opponents, lulled African suspicions, and trumped the Kenya settlers. It is just as well that Britain quitted Kenya but it could have been arranged with more honesty and less 'shrewdness'. By 1968 Macleod suddenly discovered 'moral pledges' to the Asians of East Africa which must have made sad reading for such of the elderly Kenya second-lieutenants as were still alive. Their Boy Scout self-images had been sacrificed to that of the bridge-player. And judging from the massive abstentions by millions of Conservative voters in the 1964 and 1966 General Elections, others felt let down too.

Labour profited by the staleness of the country's mood but once in office dragged out its old resentful images and as a result precipitated an even worse economic crisis. Wilson may have started off with the notion expressed by his party's last outstanding scholar: 'The best type of Cabinet Minister is a really intelligent man of the world who can think rapidly and in an orderly way.'[4] But after the commission of one major error of judgement after another in every field of policy, the mirror on the wall of Number Ten must by 1970 have been giving answers as evasive as Wilson's own. And in the meantime he encouraged

[4] H. J. Laski, *Parliamentary Government in England* (Allen and Unwin, 1959), p. 289.

the Parliamentary Labour Party to indulge in what has probably been the most prolonged orgy of moral posturing and scapegoat hunting in British politics. By the time some three-quarters of the governments of the world (particularly those run by Europeans or those of European descent) had been denounced as Fascists or racialists and Labour had run out of Africans as images of virtue, some form of hangover might have been expected. However, right up to the General Election of 1970, debates on foreign affairs were still conducted on the assumption that Britain had the means and the standing to lay down a moral law to all mankind.

So in British politics as conducted with present slogans and personalities we can only look forward to the continual tarnishing of self-imagery while the Opposition waits until the party in office has got so stale that it will be turned out. How long can we go on like this? Even if most government business is a matter of management, the managers have still to represent themselves to the electorate as something more than managers and the 'something more' must be either demonstrated by their qualities as men (and on the whole this produces the best sort of government) or by appearing to be the embodiment of some idea. If they cannot demonstrate one or the other, unease spreads among the managed who although they are supposed to like their rulers to be 'just like themselves' in fact set store by the illusion of being governed by their 'better' selves.

This is surely the classic situation for the intellectual to step in and provide society with an idea of such overpowering attraction that consciousness would fasten on it in the hope of finding a new certainty of identity and the politicians would abandon their old shop-soiled goods for the sake of selling the new line to the electorate. But though it is two hundred years since Rousseau handed out his version of Man as a gift to academics and demagogues, he refuses to die. The spell of his *Confessions* works even on those who have never read them. Since he never quite made the milieu of the wealthy and polite, he has bequeathed to posterity the classic role of the intellectual as a potential member of an élite ready at the drop of a social contract to step into the tyrant's shoes and lay down his version of Natural Law for us all. Since his conscience is infallible, his view of his fellow-men will be as ferocious as that of Hitler. His modern counterparts, having found their *neveu de Rameau* in various louche Africans and Latin Americans, have settled on a vague imperialism-cum-capitalism-cum-America-cum-social convention as the 'society' which is responsible for their 'crime'. This is irrelevant for policy-making.

Considering the upturn mankind has been through over the past sixty years, the Western intellectual effort to reinterpret the deep springs of human consciousness and reassess motives and patterns of political behaviour has been extremely feeble. Sociologists produce wordy theses about group patterns in minor fields, the Lévi-Strauss version of the notion that primitive man can furnish us with the secret of the universal mind is not much of an advance over Herder, and Noam Chomsky produces a numerical variant of the standard working hypothesis of comparative philologists that language may reveal the basic structure of thought, while their colleagues write them up as new and daring thinkers. The profound reappraisal which the still largely inexplicable phenomenon of Naziism should have brought about is discussed in terms of a Right and Left which never existed. The more general question of 'Fascism', which outside Germany was largely a question of power politics linked to a rag-bag of Central and Eastern European local issues, is as dangerously misrepresented to-day as it was in the thirties. As Mr. Tibor Szamuely has pointed out: 'What do the following have in common: Harold Wilson, Nguyen Cao Ky, Charles de Gaulle, Enoch Powell, George Papadopoulos, Anthony Crosland, Georges Bidault, T. S. Eliot, Barry Goldwater, Axel Springer, and the Shah of Persia? Two things: first, they have all, at different times in the recent past, been called fascists (sometimes by each other) and secondly, none of them have ever been fascists in any recognizable sense of the word.'[5]

So any attempt by the so-called intellectual New Left to redefine Universal Man in terms of his Enemy Number One is bound to be as far off the mark as it ever was with the Old Left. The rebel poets and intellectuals of the thirties, now barely recognizable as a gaggle of grey-haired queenies in the Royal Opera House crush bar, satisfied themselves that they had emancipated themselves with words and passion is spent anyhow. The youngest generation on the other hand seems to be feeling the emotional strain of being emancipated and may well be looking for someone to repress them. Their language may still be that of emancipation: their need could be for authority. Instead of looking for a cure, we make a cult of the disease and the twentieth-century version of the *jeunesse en pleurs* has to indulge in even

[5] 'Fascism Then And Now.' Article in *Spectator,* 21.6.68.

more extravagant forms of revolt in its attempts to make itself interesting.

Nor are the professional historians very helpful—at least not in Britain. None of them seems to be able to take up even a half-stance outside the process: in fact their Programme Three appearances oblige them to show that they are 'with' the process. Professor Toynbee's psychic spirals of history correspond more to some spiralling of his own mind than to *wie es wirklich war*. Seeking a rebuttal of dogmatic Whig or ecclesiastical versions of history, Professor Trevor-Roper makes a cult of Franco-Scottish eighteenth-century sceptics. The human dilemmas of the past naturally appeal to C. V. Wedgwood's sense of female compassion. Dr. E. J. Hobsbawn turns from the economic causes of revolt to produce a book on banditry just as the revolting young are becoming bored with dialectical materialism and are taking up the cult of violence for violence's sake. With unashamed nostalgia Sir Arthur Bryant sees Europe's historical identity as a tale of banners, titles, and trumpet calls, while at the opposite extreme H. J. Plumb produces a most unconvincing account of how the myths of the past were used to exploit the loyalties of the masses and now we must shake them off to 'achieve our identity, not as Americans or Russians, Chinese or Britons, black or white, rich or poor, but as men'.[6] A most unhistorical crowd in fact and although they and their American colleagues work on the general assumption that Europe's history is one of emancipation, political authoritarianism and not democracy continues to be the most widespread and enduring form of government. 'The mind must be free or the arts perish' is a trite enough phrase but in historical perspective they seem to have flourished impartially under both authoritarianism and democracy. As the late J. H. Huizinga wrote, the course of European history is best explained as a 'tendency in the spirit of the age to recreate in real life an ideal image of the past'.[7]

So what do we create out of the spirit of our own age? Those who affect to hear the croaking of Odin's ravens, see Britain entering its Weimar period. This too is only wilful self-projection since the circumstances of Weimar can never be duplicated. There can of course be vaguely reminiscent surface patterns of behaviour: the New Left and their immature hangers-on may behave like the Nazi provo-

[6] *The Death of the Past* (Macmillan, 1969), p. 145.
[7] *Men and Ideas* (Eyre & Spottiswoode, 1960), p. 197.

cateurs from 1929 when the Allied evacuation of the Rhineland made it safe for them to appear in public. British Governments show the same hesitancy in coping with violence on the streets, buggery has been legalized, and permissiveness is in the air. But this does not make Weimar.

If a German analogy has any relevance it will rather be found in Wilhelmine Germany where the sensitive members of society began to develop a sense of suffocation. What began as intellectual and aesthetic discontents turned after 1918 into complete disintegration under the impact of defeat and revolution. The reversal of second-order factors, of those special conditions which determined the historical forms of German society, was too complete. The first-order factors which operate on basic consciousness itself, particularly the human need for participation, emerged as forces which no one had foreseen but which Hitler knew how to exploit. The error was that of the 'progressive' Germans who in their blueprints for a new society prior to 1918 had lumped all human motives and characteristics into one category of causes, inevitably labelled 'Man'. And to-day the malaise of Britain, the United States, probably of France and to a lesser degree other European countries, arises from ideas which can only be sustained at the price of falsehood and from institutions which can only be maintained by the betrayal of men. If now crisis breaks or disaster strikes, it is important that we do not make the same error and that our image of Man does not blind us to the make-up of men.

If universality implies brushing aside the second-order factors which determine local identity, it is to be expected that there will be signs of disintegration within the framework of liberal-humanitarian ideas built up on the notion of an emancipated Man with his corollary of universal equality. Nor is it enough to counter permissiveness with cries about human dignity when the material drives of society itself involve the destruction of the sense of the fitting and its replacement by unbounded appetite. And in an era of inversion emotional intensity can bring about nasty convergences; sensitivity and brutality can recombine as not only the Germans have demonstrated. The wistful Lawrences would put aside their books of sonnets to help their local guerillas set up some new devilish form of death trap. If we all come under pressure to model ourselves on some fantasy character, the effort to restore our own will can be too great and we have to fall back on *ersatz* images, whether Cuban or Carnaby Street in origin. We are at once inverted and can never be ourselves. So the phenomenon is a form of neurosis and the emotion which we shall increasingly transfer to the objects will be that of hate. It was bad enough having Young Werther blowing out his own brains but even worse if he starts blowing out those of everyone else.

Europe's passion for objectivation has thus by a strange paradox become self-preoccupation. Every form of nature carries in it some element or quality which will prove destructive once it begins to predominate. 'He's ower self-conscious, that yin,' they used to say disapprovingly of some fascinating character in one's early world so that one immediately tried to make his acquaintance and was doubtless preserved only by childhood innocence from contamination. But within a generation the wheel seems to have turned full circle and 'that yin's' problem has become that of society at large. The self-consciousness which made us truly human could thus end our span.

But we have no other course than to accept the irreversible nature of the present stage. The solution in philosophic terms must be to find some means of detaching ourselves from the present objects of consciousness and finding new ones round which the subject can rebuild a new sense of objectivity. If universality is the problem then it is from the particular that we must start out to restore the sense of the fitting and set up those *images de comportment* which, as Bertrand de Jouvenel suggests, determine the quality of institutions and the manner in which power is exercised.

Fortunately the process remains uneven. The seventies will bring tensions and clashes at least as great as, and probably greater than, those of the sixties. Technological, economic, educational, strategic and racial factors will force dislocation and conflict. The Russians, who can keep their introversion in a separate compartment of the mind, will continue with their calculated exploitation of external power factors wherever they sense weakness or confusion among their potential enemies. And the second-order factors which created Europe's particularities have not all disappeared even if the English seem most determined to destroy their own identity.

And we have still to take into account the impact of the non-European world. For Euro-centric universalism will not be allowed to continue in its present form. Self-consciousness has also set in among other races and cultures with consequences which cannot be foreseen. Nor have we yet experienced all the circumstances which can arise from trying to operate a balance of power under the threat of universal destruction. In Europe, periods of great fear have been preludes to persecution, to terror, and the distorted escapisms of religious fanaticism. The tasks of rulers will not become easier and their successes or failures will offer new objective possibilities of power; and to quote De Jouvenel again: 'Ce n'est pas pour l'homme; c'est pour le Pouvoir qu'en dernière analyse sont faites les révolutions.'[8]

There will therefore be pressures, probably disagreeable ones, which will call for outward action and compel us to abandon our escapist or neurotic images. But action on the scale required to give society a combined sense of liberation and of solidarity will open up awesome prospects of power. How can we ensure that it will not be put to the service of the fantasies of Young Werther—or Young Adolf? For successful action immediately validates an idea and before we realize it we are being dragged along in the wake of yet another monolithic obsession. But short of the impact of some completely external catastrophe which would restore the older naïve human relationships by making us face the grimmest necessities of survival, this is a risk which will have to be taken. 'In the beginning', said Faust, 'was the deed.' And it will also be the deeds which have the last word.

---

[8] *Du Pouvoir* (Éditions du Cheval Ailé, 1947), p. 286.

F

IV. The Duce was Right

IV. The Duce was Right

The florid calls to action of the Italian Fascist era were not wrong as conceptions. The Duce was right—in rhetoric. 'Better to live a day like lions than a thousand years like sheep.' 'Combat not discussion.' 'Conquer, Conquer, Conquer.' The slogans can still be deciphered under the smudges of post-war democratic overpainting. The Italians enjoyed repeating them and Mussolini, who was by profession a Socialist leader-writer, was good at coining them. But when the time came for action, no one was prepared to stick his neck out and the Duce's capacity for judging when and how to act proved to be non-existent. It was the wrong call for action for the wrong people.

The disasters of the Nazi-Fascist interlude have consequently added to the disrepute into which authority and power had already fallen in liberal political thought. If our view of our fellow-men is little more than a series of projections of self-imagery, we may well wonder whether there can be any safe guides to action. So far from finding courses which bolster up society's sense of security, we may merely be adding to our fellow-citizen's insecurity by projecting round us our own feelings of inadequacy. Fear of power thus becomes its own justification, and those most active in laying bare and denouncing evidence of neo-Fascism appear to find their supporting arguments in their own resentments.

In our century the acts of will which went into shaping the various philosophies of action certainly affected the will to act of others in ways different to those intended by their authors. Marxist mystiques of group action have produced a baleful progeny of authoritarian élitism. Collectivist absolutism has proved to be the outcome of movements professing concern for civil liberty, much to the confusion of their loyal followers. By a happier paradox the corporate institutions of Fascism initiated Italians into the art of managing large-scale industrial enterprise in partnership with the State, how on one hand to develop the modalities of working relationships between government departments and private bodies and how on the other to maintain a rule-of-thumb balance between overall investment, production, and consumption. The deed is decisive although its outcome is often unexpected.

As we emerged from the consequences of the Nazi era, we naturally started querying the assumptions on which we believed our whole European civilization had rested. A hesitancy in facing issues of authority, a diffidence in offering opinions over obvious differences in human capacity, an exaggerated regard for the susceptibilities of Jews although they doubtless have their proportionate share of human shortcomings, and an over-anxiety about the *Schweinhund* who may be lurking in all of us. All these doubts add up to an inhibition about certain types of action or even about thoughts which point to action. And without action our doubts can only increase.

The appeal of Fascism in the thirties, although this is now forgotten —so quickly does the past fade—was that its leaders put forward the plausible claim that they got things done and gave Italians, Germans, and Spaniards the illusion that they were escaping from situations which they felt had become intolerable. And if the demagogue playing on the wide keyboard of irrationality managed to achieve a mass following in any European society, this would again be his most effective slogan and the rout would again be led by those who had locked themselves in an intellectual muddle about the legitimacy of authority and the practical issues of power. Even if there were no mass of ex-storm troopers ready to relive their days of action and no real or imagined wide-felt national grievances, there would still be the excitement of rediscovering emotional unity and the satisfaction of feeling that the break between governors and governed had been healed. There would be a promise of new experience and new knowledge.

This need for participation is not a mere throw-back to the animal herd; nor are brass bands, flags, and jackboots basic to its appeal. It is an essential element in evolving human consciousness. During the millenia before men could write down or parse their thoughts, they sensed that 'to be able' was 'to know'. The usage of these verbs in language indicates their common origin in purposeful action; the common derivation of both is the human intuition that capability and knowledge are identical in practice. However self-conscious we may be about our heritage of language, the disciplines of formal verbalization still do not prevent our thoughts slipping readily if ungrammatically from 'können' to 'kennen', from the cunning to the knowing. For the oldest human wisdom discovered the reality of objects in their use and not in their appearance, and that without purposeful usage there could be no knowing.

Only when we try to apply to objects those verbal descriptions which we flatter ourselves are 'pure thought' do appearances become deceptive and academic philosophers start talking about pseudo-problems. But when the world of objects is treated as a theatre of action, no problem either real or pseudo arises as to its nature, for straight away Europeans seek to extend their environment of purpose —into the bowels of the earth, into the smallest particles of inorganic and organic matter, and into outer space. The theological arguments about the nature of the universe backed up by scholarship and logic collapse under the utilitarian test of the telescope, the microscope, and the moon rocket. It will not be otherwise with our institutions and institutionalized ideas.

The virtue hitherto claimed for the British political system was that authority was transmitted by tribal qualities of *esprit de corps*, leadership, and loyalty, as produced by region, school, regiment, professional adherence, or traditional grouping, so that power and action were little more than instinctive reactions and for their legitimacy rarely required formal conceptual reassessment. Since our society provides an increasingly unfavourable environment for the development or even survival of these qualities, there may have to be for the first time in British political history formal definitions of the nature of men's relationships in society: without this, effective communal action may eventually become impossible.

The political significance of the Suez misadventure of 1956 was that it was the last self-conscious fling of the old British style. Its failure may even have been mainly due to this style having become over self-conscious: the play and not the reality was the thing. As the old wartime basements in Whitehall were opened up for the task-force planners, they all flocked in—the Lawrences of Groppi and Shepheards—rather too puffy of face and corpulent of body to play wistful roles. They were nevertheless delighted to see each other again, swap old memories, and once more sport their D.S.O.s, M.C.s and *Croix de Guerre*. The phoney brigadiers who had once run phoney outfits in Cairo were there too, trying to find excuses for upping their rank to Major-General. Julian Amery came round with news of plots and conspiracies and Colonel Neil Maclean hurried from the Commons to ask to be sent on a delicate, difficult, or dangerous mission: he was offered one and to his credit carried it out admirably.

For the Prime Minister it was the heaven-sent opportunity he had been seeking to rally the loyalty and respect of his colleagues and party which he had sensed, without knowing why and wherefore, were lacking. Here was an enemy who could demonstrably be defeated and a sanctimonious American Secretary of State whose duplicity could be exposed. The analogies with the pre-war appeasement of dictators were post-decision rationalization.

There were disturbing accompanying symptoms. One service chief washed his hands of the whole affair while another sat disconsolately in the wings as Eden assembled a group of force commanders whose conduct of the expedition was only too predictable. And even more troubling was the emergence in Whitehall of little cliques who went round saying: Is it moral? It had always been a fascinating game to speculate who in 1940 would have been on Dover quay to offer his services to the Gauleiter of Gross-Britannien and with what arguments he would have justified himself. Now one knew.

The collapse of the expedition left a malaise which has carried over into another generation. It may be fashionable at the moment to query how widespread was patriotic feeling at the turn of the century but the British, more than any other nation of the Western world, did develop their remarkable sense of Britishness largely as a result of their foreign adventures, wars, conquests, explorations, and missions. By the time imperialism and even jingoism had become the fashion in political oratory and popular literature, the national pride of the majority of English and Scots, some of the Irish, and even a few of the Welsh, had come to centre round overseas feats of arms and men. Imperialism was effect rather than cause: Dean Acheson may only have been half-right. Nevertheless the Suez action was regarded as a national action—the last of its kind—and its failure has been sensed as a national failure.

The continuing malaise is that of an emptiness. The subsequent successful armed confrontation of Soekarno meant little to the generality nor was there any widely felt chagrin over our withdrawals from Africa and Southern Arabia. While the man in the pub reacts vaguely to reports of Middle Eastern turmoil with 'Eden was right' and leaves it at that, our active political participants seem to be unable to accept that the expedition meant the end of British power and influence in the region. The Labour back-benchers, who cry 'Suez' at any Tory attempt to define an overseas British national interest, are still the most active in laying down what should be done to settle Middle Eastern conflicts. The various protagonists of Jew and Arab rage at each other without anything they say having the slightest effect on events. Mr. (now Lord) George-Brown buzzed round the Levant like a bumble bee in a bottle and Neil Maclean prowls about the wilder shores in search of wars and uprisings occasionally emerging in Kurdistan, Muscat, or Eritrea with tommy gun under his arm and looking puzzled rather than wistful. Other appeals to action—to aid the underdeveloped, to support the United Nations, to boycott Rhodesians, or demonstrate hostility to South Africans—leave the British unmoved.

Since Suez, British Governments have shown a curious inability to select courses of action which are not only within our capacity to sustain but are even necessary if we are to sustain our capabilities. Macmillan's policy of 'keeping our heads down', which became the fashionable Whitehall phrase in the post-Suez demoralization, ended in drift, indifference, and cynicism throughout the Whitehall establishment of administrators and service chiefs and has even infected high finance and big business. Wilson's period of pseudo-activity made them even more cynical. The sad thing is that in the late fifties and early sixties Britain's power and influence *vis-à-vis* Western Europe and the Middle East were still sufficient to enable us to choose independent and constructive lines of policy had we wanted. *Vis-à-vis* the United States and Russia they were minimal: there could thus be nothing 'special' about our relationship with the Americans and we could no more be a mediator between them and the Soviet Bloc than could Liechtenstein.

Yet this was the course of non-action which Macmillan chose to follow. Some realization of his error began to dawn when Dulles vetoed his journeyings to Moscow, and when the State Department indicated that it expected to be informed every time we moved a platoon of infantry, and finally demanded and obtained a *suppressio veritati* in British policy statements on issues such as Cuba, Indonesia, and the Congo. But by then Macmillan either could not or dare not stop his great mediating act and in Whitehall frank discussion of American factors was forbidden by Cabinet circular. And so the self-deception of Ministers had to be supported by others lying to each other and to themselves. Finally in December 1962 there was a sort of jumble sale of odds and ends of remaining British sovereignty, beginning with defence planning and weapons development, including a number of confused corollaries the significance of which we only began to discover in 1970 when we found that we could not even use our own plutonium in our own power stations without American permission.

Economic affairs followed the same drift. The 1961 International Monetary Fund consultations in Vienna's *hofburg* laid down in practice certain broad limits for British financial policy, which represented as decisive a limitation on our sovereignty as if we had surrendered some of the country's law-making functions to a supra-national body. Wilson completed the process. His economic failure resulted in the last remnants of financial sovereignty being handed over to the United States Federal Reserve Board, the German Bundesbank, and the I.M.F.: the British economy must now proceed at a pace and within limits decided by those who underwrite our reserves. Wilson's foreign policy, whether peace-making efforts in Viet-Nam or Nigeria or attempts to break Rhodesian will, seemed almost deliberately designed to show up Britain's mondial impotence.

Yet with both Macmillan and Wilson it was a failure of judgement, not of power. For British military and economic ascendancy began its relative decline a hundred years ago with the rise of Germany and the United States and the falling-off of French power. The decline was concealed by our apparent ability to bring in counter-balancing factors to strengthen what became an Anglo-French common position —first Russia, then Empire and Commonwealth, and finally the United States. But in none of these moves were the power factors identical and the military effectiveness of such combinations depended on the goals and the strategic requirements. Instinct and calculation determined the policy decisions, and the oratory and imagery associated with them from Burke to Churchill gained their credibility from the success of action and not the other way round. The British failures of the last two decades derive from this misapprehension, leaving a paralysis of will at the policy-making level of Whitehall and also contributing to the Westminster complot by which Government and Opposition sought to avoid decisions on the most important questions of the day by 'taking them out of politics'.

So if they are now searching for a programme of action which will restore their own self-confidence and then inspire confidence in others, the Conservatives have in the foreign-policy field to distinguish between effective power factors and those which are as mythical as our own self-imagery. The attraction of 'Europe', whether the totality of its peoples or the narrower conception of the Common Market, is that it appears to offer a field of action with an attainable goal at the end. But shall we be only exchanging one myth for another and how good are the 'Europeans' themselves at distinguishing between the real and the mythical when action calls?

By 1939 the French had arrived at a state of mind analogous to the present British one. Their politicians' antics had become meaningless in terms of national interest, the official establishment was cynical and defeatist, and the individual washed his hands of any public responsibility and withdrew into a hard shell of selfishness. The French officer corps was less concerned with the defence of metropolitan territory than with preserving the advantages and lucrative posts which accrued to it from the army's dominating position in overseas dependencies and protectorates. But the oratorical myths persisted: France was the home of liberty and tolerance, combining a heroic martial tradition with one of creative culture. In fact France had become an island of ignorance and boorishness run by a rigid authoritarian bureaucracy. The truth may have been sensed by some but not until 1958 did the majority of the metropolitan French admit what may have been in their hearts for three decades and accept that autocracy was the best system for them: not until General Salan's abortive coup did the army ascendancy beat its final retreat.

The De Gaulle interlude was a skilful management of French membership of alliances for its nuisance value. It was only effective up to the point where France ceased to have a value and became a nuisance: the impact on non-Allies such as Russia, China, and Latin America was illusory. Starry military dreams came up against the astronomical costs of modern weapon systems. De Gaulle's mystical self-identification with France turned to pique when things started to go wrong.

But May 1968 did not produce a revolution: this misreading of the events only reflected Left-Wing myth-making. For hard work and selfishness have brought prosperity to the majority. The university and lycée troubles turned out to be little more than a large-scale *chahut* and the industrial workers who profited by the preoccupations of authority to strike for higher wages firmly resisted any association with the students. The significant clue was the dog that failed to bark: the French Communist Party remained outwardly inactive in spite of its following and its hold on the loyalties of a central core of workers. For the P.C.F. has one role—to remain in being against the day of action which will be decided in Moscow. The intellectual purges of the Party in 1969 and 1970 were the outward expression of the cold determination of the P.C.F. leadership to maintain its authority: they have bigger game in their sights. Meanwhile prefectural rule will continue, the so-called student rebels of May 1968 will be the materialist boors and potential collaborators of tomorrow, and the French army will break and run if an external threat of the order of June 1940 again looms. The changed emphasis in France after a decade of De Gaulle is that the P.C.F. is more disciplined than ever and that the French people as a whole are prepared to accept open authoritarianism. The individual Frenchman will remain in his hard selfish shell and his national cuisine will continue to deteriorate.

In the same way, the Italian Communists, the largest single party in their country, bide their time as they watch Centre and Right fumble and fail. With ample funds and effective publicists the P.C.I. acquires a new aura of authority as the Italian in the street senses that coalition politics are increasingly divorced from his family interests and worries about the growing spasmodic violence of the towns. The very success of Italian capitalism over the post-war period has brought about what the economic crises of the twenties and thirties did not—the radicalization of the Italian masses and a greater readiness for the confrontation forecast by Palmiro Togliatti and Luigi Longo. The long doctrinal argument with Moscow, seeking permission to produce the appearance of an independent dialectic suited to the Italian political scene, may now be paying off. As the authority of the Catholic Church crumbles, the older regional bonds dissolve within the new industrial framework; and the same process is happening in Spain. The Romance-speaking countries of Western Europe are moving to a new crisis of loyalty where the challenge of action could be in Communist hands. The Communists may fumble too and other Italians and Spaniards have also retained their guile, while the Russians may misjudge the situation in 1973 as they did in Germany in 1933.

However, some of the more sensational events within the Soviet Bloc have tended to divert attention from the continuity of ideas and the power of personal authority exercised over long periods of time. Does it matter if the Russian model in itself no longer appears applicable in other countries? If Russian power requires instruments and if ambitious men need backers, they will find occasion for joint action. The democratic liberation causes of the nineteenth century were for many decades useful tools in the service of Great Power politics, however shoddy may have been the performance of democrats in office.

Action can therefore bring about the *commutatio* of a whole move-ment. If thirty years ago we believed that liberalism still had roots in France and had lost them in Germany, to-day's possibility that it is the other way round should bring home how imperfect and super-ficial is our grasp of the shifting process of political ideas and loyalties. German liberals and socialists were for some sixty years significant political forces until they succumbed as overt movements to external coercion in 1933. They have re-emerged after fifteen years of Naziism and war had destroyed the social foundation on which the older authoritarian habits of German administration had been based. But these years had also destroyed the German sense of pride, honour, and service, which were inherent in the older system. To-day's living generation of Germans cannot therefore share the motives of the conspirators of 1944. German liberalism to-day may be too open-minded, too ready to offer itself to any cause affecting to profess related ideals, while the pride, honour, and service which are still needs of men in society are absent. Hagen could get the upper hand.

And the new *Ostpolitik* carries its own risks. The belief that by playing so far with the Russians some progress can be made towards the reunification of a divided people places a powerful psychological weapon in Kremlin hands, which the Russians would not hesitate to use at the strategic juncture; that is to say, when circumstances in France, Italy, and Spain combined with domestic weakness or dissension in the United States provided a propitious opening for action. *Die deutsche Treue* rests on too uncertain a basis for us to be sure how a German government—or governments—would react to the agonizing choices or enticing offers which would be pressed upon the German people: the influential voices of those who have developed a vested interest in the *Ostpolitik* would serve Russia just as well as a Communist movement. The pledges of alliance throughout Western Europe would feel the strain of power moves which could expose NATO as being as impotent as it was in 1953 in East Germany, in 1956 in Hungary, and in 1968 in Czechoslovakia. Russia moves first, presents a *fait accompli*, and afterwards produces her justification, well aware that she will find helpful advocates to describe her actions as 'an objective factor of history'.

To this, under the Treaty of Rome, Western Europe opposes an action programme holding forth the promise of a powerful institutiona-lized grouping of states, with a population and a productive capacity far beyond anything Russia can hope to achieve before the end of the century. But it is still only a promise, a distant goal of a common interest which has yet to supersede the sectional selfishness of French and Italians, Walloons and Flemings, and fully commit the resources and interests of Germany. The process of creating the European Economic Community in the face of setbacks and diversions is essentially that of creating institutions for directing economic power. In this it resembles the process of founding the Greek *polis* since it is entirely calculating and rational in its character, even when older intuitive and emotional problems are involved such as the ordering of Europe's peasant communities with their tribal and traditional past. The perfect solution may not yet be in sight but, unlike the United States Constitution, the Treaty of Rome is at least blessedly free of semi-theological evocations or of romantic advocacy.

But while the Treaty of Rome can provide an inner defensive line, tomorrow's need may also be for resolute external action for which the North Atlantic Treaty Organisation, as at present constituted, provides no design, while the shifting nature of the Russo-American confrontation has only changed the potential nature of conflict without reducing its likelihood. Western Europe faces the risk that the two Great Powers may on occasion have to act first in their own interest and Europeans will find that they have no say in the consequences. As Russia grows in material power and America suffers from the impact of a sense of unfulfilment in her foreign ventures and from the erosion of her domestic institutions, the situation changes for those in No Man's Land.

So although the theory of stalemate through mutual deterrence still prevails in higher strategy, Russia has found new openings for action and in so doing creates new factors which invalidate the old assumptions. Through proxies, through supply of conventional weapons and through the occasional display of her own land, sea, and air forces, she has steadily undermined Western positions which a decade ago we should have expected could be challenged only by all-out threats of war. Russian power is visible in several oceans and the Cuban reversal of 1962 has been made good by the appearance in the Caribbean of a Russian naval squadron complete with missile-launchers, landing craft, and marines. All the Americans can do is to try to convince the Russians of the reality of their potential local counter-power— with moderate success.

Western Europe may find itself part of a similar 'local situation' where the outcome will depend on its own capacity for independent action. But here too are myths to be dispelled, such as the notion of an 'independent nuclear deterrent'. The claims that its possession would give any European state a say in Russo-American exchanges were never more than political self-delusion by Macmillan and De Gaulle and have never been taken seriously by any American or Russian leader. There is nothing, Charles Lamb reminded us, so irrelevant as a poor relation.

If Western Europe, including Britain, hopes to be able to reshape its institutions to its own, rather than to some outsider's liking, it has two immediate tasks. First it has to produce a new concept of external politico-strategic action, probably more political than military, and secondly it has to make certain choices concerning the quality of its society if it is to hold internal loyalties. It will be a sad British society which is excluded from the debate on Europe's longer-term aims. The *Rechtsstaat* basis of European political life means that the debate and its outcome could be as rich in constitutional precedent and practice as with the United States a century and a half ago: and in an age when modern techniques themselves are liable to become instruments for controlling every physical and mental aspect of the human organism, we dare not deny ourselves any opportunity for political knowing and cunning. If the debate is not resolved Europe may enter an age of turbulence as dangerous as it has ever faced in its history and there will be pressures from without as well as from within which could bring it to its knees.

So if power has its dangers, an aversion to applying power leaves an even more dangerous gap in human relations. It is possible that Europeans may seek to evade the risks by the same sort of escapism which British politicians followed in the thirties. Even in the fifties and sixties we followed this escape route, proclaiming that we had a special role in 'world leadership' while those who were supposed to be setting examples of purposeful action merely launched vacuous calls for a sense of national purpose. This has now been going on since the twenties with only a wartime break.[1] When action is evaded or

---

[1] 'The airy neglect of the significance of power which has marked English liberal thought for the last fifty years soon ceased to be a mere adornment. By an astonishing process of permeation, it came to dominate both the Labour Movement and, even more remarkable, the Conservative Party as well. Mr. Amery became a back number because he refused to renounce common sense; and Mr. Baldwin, Mr. Eden, and Lord Halifax entered on the inheritance of the British imperial tradition. Converted by the phrases

blurred, the limits of authority itself become increasingly ambiguous
and ill-defined so that a new threat to the liberties of the citizenry
comes into being. The permissiveness which results from the failure
of law-enforcement ultimately defeats itself when, as in the Weimar
Republic, those who suffer from resentments increasingly begin to
take the law into their own hands. In the end too much tolerance
breeds intolerance.

In this situation, action at least does start its catalysis and in
some future context of history this may be seen as the one fruitful
role of the contemporary members of society whose extreme or unhappy
attitudes at present cause us so much concern. Instinct can be too
much outraged by invalid ideas and sensitive and serious people are
suffering almost physically from the inability to find a new framework
of ideas to give coherence to daily human experience. Unfortunately
those who should be helping them have turned the malady into a
justification. And while random violence may interrupt normal and
predictable personal or social patterns of behaviour, it does not thereby
become creative action and since it is random it can neither validate
nor invalidate any idea. It will not even expose 'the violence which is
at the basis of society', to use the modish Leftish jargon. All that random
violence establishes is that those who outlaw themselves by arbitrary
acts will be treated as outlaws while those who endeavour to act
within the framework of laws continue with their own assumptions.
The contemporary violent protestors console themselves that in terms
of some vague Marxist determinism and at some indeterminate
point in the future, 'history' will be seen to have been on their side
and therefore their arbitrariness possesses its own morality. However,
Mussolini and Hitler also claimed to have history on their side, and so
it appeared for some years until it went over to someone else's side. If
Lenin saw violence as the handmaid or the midwife of history, this
was still as part of a rationale. The present notions stand up to no
form of rational test and produce no evidence for their validity.
Sexual liberation and social revolution are said to be causally linked

---

of the League of Nations Union (an important electoral factor), they too
began to denounce "power politics" and to believe that the status quo could
be defended by high-minded appeals to "the rule of law" and "the sanctity
of treaties" combined with an equally high-minded surrender to threats of
force.' R. H. S. Crossman, *The Charm of Politics* (Hamish Hamilton, 1958),
pp. 92–3.

but this is borne out by no revolution in history. While the New Left still advances the theory that the proletarian class is committed to an anti-capitalist revolution, the only workers' revolutionary movements of the past three decades, in East Germany, Hungary, and Czechoslovakia, have been directed against Communist regimes.

Without a coherent basis, the New Left movement cannot for long hold a widespread loyalty; it appeals at most to loose or shifting associations or to age groups attracted by a passing fad. Its persistent elements can only drift into other dissident groups, often professing opposing views, so that the pacifists and disarmers of a decade ago are now associated with violence and wars. The action groups deteriorate into ever more amorphous collections of drop-outs, drug addicts, and psychopaths, rather as the nineteenth-century anarchists finished up as café absinthe drinkers, their talk becoming ever more incoherent as their elbows and trouser seats wore out.

But the longer-term effect of this unexpected catalysis is now becoming apparent: it is bringing about the discrediting of the liberal attempt to write off the need for power. This is not a reaction to be written off as some local 'backlash' of indignant citizens. It is now almost forgotten history that the whole New Left movement got its first major impetus from the encouragement given to civil-rights demonstrators by President Kennedy and his brother Robert, then U.S. Attorney-General, as part of their attempt to maintain the pretence of being a 'liberal' administration. At the time it seemed a good gimmick. But the peace movement blessed by the Kennedy brothers blossomed out into a pro-Communist hate campaign while civil rights have now become the shooting and bombings of Black Panthers and Weathermen. The Marcuse thesis of 'repressive tolerance' was followed to its logical conclusion in the New Left campus-debate argument that the higher morality of protest requires the suppression of individual rights and free speech, and by the campus itself being taken over by outside activists. Professor Marcuse's 'best student', the negress Angela Davis, was by January 1971 appearing on charges of murder, kidnapping and buying the weapons used in a courtroom battle when a judge was killed.

The anarchic movements have done more than anything else to revive the issue of the legitimacy of institutions and their relationship to human identity. '. . . All we know is that the sense of institutions being legitimate—especially the institutions of government—is the glue that holds societies together. When it weakens, things become

G

unstuck.'[2] And since American fashions tend to be taken up in Britain, we have experienced a suitably modified form of the same course of events and consequences. Unmindful of the fate of the Kennedy brothers, justification for violent spasmodic student and other demonstrations was quite gratuitously handed out by Wilson and his Ministers. However, the British student troubles have not been linked to any national issue which concerns or embarrasses wider sections of society. That they have taken place at all is due rather to the indulgence of teachers, wardens, and parents than to any genuine passion of strength in the movements. To quote Professor Alasdair MacIntyre, it was 'the first parent-financed revolt in what is more like a new version of the children's crusade than a revolutionary movement'.[3]

But the consequence has again been to posit the issue of legitimate authority which would normally have been ignored with the usual British assumption that it can't happen here. This rested on two premises which are no longer tenable—first that the stable, almost placid temperament of a homogenous British people can be counted upon to maintain traditional customs and institutions, and second that, unlike the United States, widespread crime would never be a way of life. But the homogeneity is on the verge of disappearing to be replaced in those main urban centres, where the daily habits of society are formed, by a mixture of races with incompatible cultures and a large detribalized and proletarianized negro element. Meantime the upward graph of criminal statistics, while terrifying enough in itself, does not reveal the growing component of well-organized professional networks notably in London, Liverpool, Manchester, Leeds, Birmingham, Newcastle, Cardiff, Nottingham, and Bradford, again those same urban centres. Whatever successes are recorded by the forces of detection, the volume of unsolved crime now exceeds the number of *all* crimes which ten years ago were reported by the police.[4] The trendy ones find ready excuses. 'Apart from the factor of conviction, there are no differences between criminals and non-criminals', writes Dr. Dennis Chapman, who finds that the role of the victim in crime can be crucial and that the criminals are scapegoats to resolve the emotional conflict which arises from our general wrong-doing.[5] Be this as it

---

[2] Memo of Mr. Daniel Patrick Moynihan of 3.1.69 to President Nixon.
[3] *Marcuse* (Fontana, 1970).
[4] F. H. McClintock and N. Howard Avison, *Crime in England and Wales* (Heinemann, 1968).
[5] *Sociology and the Stereotype of the Criminal* (Tavistock Publications, 1968).

may, the continuation of present trends indicates that in default of some greater cause, there will be increasing violence and lawlessness centring round the loyalties of streets, groups, races, or gangs.

So even without an initial act of will a pattern of action is emerging which has nothing to do with the British New Left and with which the Old Left leadership, as personified in the Labour and Socialist mavericks of the thirties, cannot cope, since they have gone too far in their compromises with the forces of disruption to be able to reassert authority. And if the Conservatives cannot restore its legitimacy, the task will one day have to be undertaken as one of imposition, more likely by someone who is exploiting lowest common denominators as motives of action, than by a more fastidious nature selecting a quality such as 'Love' as the ordering principle of the universe.

Why will there assuredly be a someone? Because our instrumentalist attitude towards things will without any concept of authority be extended over our fellow-men as a desire for dominion. Like Kant we can try to postulate Man as a purpose in himself. But in practice men do use their fellows as instruments and most of all when they are sending round the fiery cross of 'human dignity'. Naturally it is their dignity which will be enhanced, not that of the men who fought, slaved, intrigued, or voted for them. But men love to share in heroic prestige and feel the reflected glory of power and if no one else can provide these, it will in the end be the paranoic, whose appetite *is* his identity and who becomes stronger as he devours, who will be elevated to power.

In European history a power vacuum has been filled sooner or later: complete emancipation would *require* a Hitler. And the first to welcome him would be the idealists who had been so assiduous in dismissing human attributes including that of will. For in their hearts they cherish that perverted worship of power in which we are exhorted to accept the *fait accompli*, give the benefit of the doubt to Brezhnev, Mao Tse-tung and Castro. If we fail to act ourselves, we do of course finish up by accepting the assumptions of those who have acted. The fear of power results in submission to power. The Duce was right!

The task now facing the Conservatives in their years of office is in theory one for which they are better suited than others, since they have a less anxious attitude about the daily business of government and in their hearts many of them have little desire to be more than managers. In so far as the Parliamentary system has shown itself to be more important than formal democracy, there is nothing wrong with this. In our own time we have had proof enough that the traditional man can relax while it has been the idealists who have been intolerant of those who do not see 'reason'. It was our 'historicism', so much denounced by Professor Sauerteig from Weissnichtwo, which aroused us against Hitlerism and enabled us to defeat it when 'reason' should have told us that we were already vanquished.

In spite of Munich there is no reason why Conservatives should feel that they are more exposed than others. The abject surrender of the Socialist Government of Prussia to Nazi bluff, the Communist connivance in the Nazi destruction of the German parliamentary system, the Jewish intellectual mockery of German habits of bourgeois decency—these were all more important in the success of the Nazi takeover than German traditionalism. And to-day it is the Left which has taken over the slogans of irrational action and the techniques of hate processions and demonstrations which were the Nazi mass weapons.

The myths now glorified by the Left differ mainly by being geographically distant rather than remote in time: the believers know just as little about the realities of what they are idealizing as did the storm troopers. Their faces develop the same sort of vacant expressions. We should hardly have expected that less than two decades after Dr. Goebbels had been busy denying Germans access to their own music, books, and drama, some of our modish writers would be forbidding the performance of their plays to South African audiences. The belief that other men can be taught lessons by denying them access to knowledge—even if apparently held by one Rector of Scotland's oldest university—reflects some twisted desire for ascendancy which goes beyond the normal liberal preference for appearing right-minded rather than being effective. And the frustrations thus revealed finally break all bounds in orgies of real or assumed guilt. Our history has had its due share of human stupidity and cruelty. But a guilt complex which can sweep aside the visible beneficent acts and accomplishments of a whole civilization, and justify the most savage barbarities of other groups of mankind, is only to be explained by some process which has dehumanized the mind.

The development of liberal habits in Britain and in the areas of British settlement—as against the authoritarianism produced by revolutionary 'liberal' politics in Continental Europe—owes less to ideals than to the presence of inherited institutions and social forms which acted as a nursery for new growths and also as a brake. The type of political self-imagery which in other lands resulted in heroic attitudes at the barricades and the throwing of round black bombs with smoking fuses was in the last century kept in check in Britain by political elements who for one reason or another were not so self-conscious. They included not only the majority of Tory and Whig aristocratic leaders, but also the ribald mob who reminded the mayor that he made his money not from his ideals but from his sarsepans. But little by little they were displaced by vocal elements whose style was whipping themselves into a verbal fury and trying to infect others with their appearance of moral frenzy. The history of British nineteenth-century party politics begins in retrospect to look like a dualism between the naïve and the narcissistic in which the latter apparently secured hold of the hustings. One unfortunate result was to force the Tory establishment into an uneasy doubling of roles in neither of which it really believed and so weaken its instinctive links with human realities.

So the Conservative leadership's task is to lead the British people back to the recognition that they themselves are the process, the institutions, and the social and economic forces, and that the appearance of external authority of the ideas and theories is illusory. The illusion has been fostered by the successive stages of the process itself. The development of party central offices, of 'leaders' elected at one remove from the electorate by the Parliamentary parties, the growth of Whitehall mandarinism over three generations since the Trevelyan reforms, the remote complexities of modern affairs—these have all supported the notion of authority/power moving on a different plane from people/delegates, so that Lord Hailsham in one Party and Mr. Michael Foot in the other do their best to present themselves as the embodiment of 'higher principles' and suggest that there are problems such as race or industrial relations which require 'higher solutions' to which human predicaments are irrelevant. The survival of the United Nations is held to take precedence over that of any of the nations constituting it, while in economic affairs attempts to impose ideal constructions of equality and 'social justice', whatever that may mean, on the random diversity of human toil and its random consequences have been little short of disastrous.

The outcome has been a general resentment where each class or section of society feels that it is being done out of something which is its due. But ideas such as equality which bear no validity in human terms are held to be immune from criticism while the discussion of an idea which might be liberating, such as inequality, is taboo. Under this weight of irrelevant objects the subject feels suffocated. So we have reached the paradox that where new rational formulation is needed in the political field, we have sought refuge in subjective imagery, while intuitive morality has hardened into a false rationalism. Since both circumstances of the paradox derive from a consciousness of self unable to come to objective terms with a changing external order, the concepts have again come to stand for their opposites.

Resolving the paradox requires a programme of action which will on one side restore to the individual a sense of personal identity and liberate him from invalid ideas and on the other assist him to recognize ideas which will secure him against arbitrariness. In other words a principle of order! Western Continental Europe has found interim relief in its programme of economic action, so that for the moment the older idealist vocabulary which accentuated inversion has tended to lapse. But since Europeans are all part of the same continuum of ideas and activities, some new definition of identity will sooner or later be required of them. In European history either the opening up of a new sphere of physical activity or the irruption of a new or revived intellectual discipline has given fresh impetus to the process, so that our consciousness has disengaged from old objects and fastened on new ones. Can we expect this? For if inner compulsion has become stronger than external challenge, we shall sit trapped, denied new knowledge and new ideals, for our idealizing too is developed by knowledge.

At some point the consequences of the invalidity of old beliefs will break in on us. No European society has ever escaped this. So the basic task of the working politician should be essentially one of recognition, spotting what is beginning to collapse in the old structure and what new structure is emerging in outline. There is always a time lag, a confusion between nostalgia for the past and the Utopia to come. Chivalry had ceased to exist by the time Chrétien de Troyes started to compose his epic poems. When Professor von Mises set out to break a lance for rugged individualism, its place had long been usurped by the Organization Man. Morality and liberty, so frequently invoked in their mythical versions, have in reality changed meaning. If all we can be certain of is that men are growing in self-consciousness, our hope must be that they are also increasing their power of self-determination. The first recognition required is perhaps that we have become unable to develop the latter capacity because the former has got out of hand.

The British problem of political recognition is less an academic than a journalistic one. It is the vocabulary of daily usage which blocks debate over courses of action and fosters narcissism: and the currency of words appears to be the property of a comparatively confined group within an extremely shallow stratum. A new institute connected with some public question is established, a new publication is launched, a new cause is proclaimed, a fresh turn of events starts off a round of correspondence in the Press and series of discussions on the wireless. But the same names and persons figure on the notepaper or on the rostrum of every public body claiming to be the supreme authority on international or economic affairs, strategic studies, race relations, overseas aid, education, or sociology. Instead of a new emergence of ideas, out comes the old vocabulary designed for self-expression rather than for practical action. Each new creation of this type widens the credibility gap between political concepts and the requirements of action.

It looks like a planned monopoly and of course it is a situation which lends itself to exploitation by small organized groups who already possess a platform. But it happens because it is a facet of a society which has neglected the effort to find new conceptual formulation for action and power, for 'being able to'. By concentrating on what we took to be 'knowing', we have opened the public forum to the verbal exhibitionist.

In theory the consequences of wrong action should be the least of our fears. For human action always brings counter-action which can offset some of the consequences of error. Even the aggressive impulse in its most destructive form has produced some of our greatest constructive advances so that we have the apparent paradox of war producing new materials, new sources of power and transport, new methods of healing, and offering the means of probing into the furthest corners of the universe. In practice there was no paradox since the extension of knowledge always means new creation for Europeans. The human story from pre-history has been one of conflict. 'Flowers are better than bullets,' said the unfortunate girl student to the National Guardsmen on Kent College campus in May 1970. So they are in gardens, in vases, and on graves. But by their violent demonstrations, the students were testing out the completely different proposition that bullets are more final than brickbats. This does not mean that an American or any other political leader must choose between flowers and bullets but that he must satisfy the human need for action, for the moment the individual enters the debatable land between community sense and mob participation, he submerges his sense of individuality. This means not just order on the campus but creating a sense of order in the mind.

So the programme of action must be supported by a valid re-statement of ideas. If the symptoms of the malady betray everywhere a sense of insecurity, the cure is theoretically a formulation of authority. But then what sort of authority? For in the liberal conception the human mind is supposed to progress by a process of emancipation from old thralls—superstition, religion, traditional conventions, economic necessity, and ignorance. The chosen instrument of eman-cipation is knowledge and if the thralls appear internal then self-knowledge is the key. To admit a need for authority is thus a regression and should be overcome, if it cannot be eradicated, by the appeal to some yet 'higher' principle. The latter however generally turns out to be of such a general nature that it offers no certain guidance in human predicaments: it is usually some wide concept such as Love, Harmony, Life-Enhancement, so that it is little more than a tautology for consciousness itself. So lacking even a claim on immortality as some sort of authoritarian reference, the completely emancipated individual is left with the same self-knowledge as Gertrude Stein's 'I am I because my little dog knows me.'

If liberal emancipation only points to personal insecurity and vacuity, we shall find that the search for a certainty principle has subconsciously begun. This is revealed when liberals start contradicting their own creed by being dogmatic about it, and when we get the topsy-turvyness of self-styled emancipators behaving like Nazis, the predikants of human dignity sponsoring the very things which are debasing human beings, and demands for state action from those who are usually most reluctant to face the implications of strong author-ity. The appeal of Marxism is that it appears to offer simultaneously a framework of authoritarian ideas, an objective analysis of factors of change, the prospect of eventual emancipation, and opportunities for immediate action. Where language lends itself to ready conceptual formulation, an appearance of verbal conciliation between the objec-tive and subjective contradictions of Marxism can be produced which will satisfy the intellectually naïve or the unscrupulous. There are sufficient of such elements within the amorphous Left which stretches from Liberals to Communists to ensure that it will be among them that treachery will be found and will find its defenders. Conservatism cannot therefore compromise with Marxism nor with ideas derived from it.

Mr. Heath began his term of office by offering what he called a new style and, as a general philosophy, proclaimed: 'We must learn to accept once again the responsibilities of living in a free society ... The fact is that the practice of true individual responsibility is the key to the well-being of the community.'[6] A White Paper on the Reorganization of Government stressed the long-term strategy of reducing the role of the State to what could be regarded as its legitimate sphere and of opening wider sectors of choice to the individual.[7] The 'British interest' was the dominant note of the first few months and doubtless a welcome change to a large section of the electorate after the 'world' and 'all mankind' themes. The new Chancellor of the Exchequer spelt out the economic philosophy in more detail: 'I believe that what is broadly termed economic freedom is essential to the wider political and social freedom which we value . . . that it is essential to the diffusion of power, to the prevention of autocracy, to the preservation and enlargement of personal choice and independence.'[8] The Home Secretary's hodge-podge of departmental functions were described as being subordinate to his 'overriding responsibility for protecting the public and ensuring the rights and liberties of the individual'.[7]

All this is a promise of freedom when British society's need is to demonstrate the legitimacy of authority and Europe's search is for an ordering principle in legitimizing new institutions. It is not wrong to give every opportunity to those who are trying by their own volition to open up new fields of endeavour, for they will generally be those who can take the lead in communal action. But it is an illusion to think that there will be a vast response to an appeal for individual responsibility and that those who have embarked on violence will suddenly acquire an inner sense of restraint. Even in the name of the 'rights and liberties of the individual' British governments are likely to be called upon to exercise authority of a firmness not known for recent decades. However, Mr. Heath was not elected to be liberal but to be conservative, and it has been suggested that the secret of the Tory Party's survival over the past century and a half has been

[6] Speech at the Guildhall, 16.11.70.

[7] H.M.S.O. Issued 16.10.70.

[8] Speech at the Mansion House, 15.10.70.

its instinct for selecting the right time to challenge the modish consensus and that this has been the primary role of Tory radicals from Young England to The Monday Club.[9]

None of these proclamations of faith need be irreconcilable with the needs of government. An ordering principle must also be a selective one and the legitimacy of state action is central to the daily functioning of administration, which is one reason—probably the chief one— why our society can never be so open as the displaced professors would like us to believe and why the rhetoric of a free society is never quite enough. Action to advance the common good requires continuous reference back to the whole body of definitions thrown up by our history.[10] In other words, it is inseparably linked to the European process of conceptualization.

Does this mean that we have to erect another great structure of ideology, with the same old risk that it will in the end result in identi-

[9] Robert Blacker *The Conservative Party: From Peel to Churchill* (Eyre & Spottiswoode, 1970), p. 271.

[10] This has been most succinctly defined by the present Head of the Home Civil Service, Sir William Armstrong, in a Commemoration Address at the London School of Economics in December 1969, which he was prevented from delivering by student wreckers. The relevant passage is: 'There is one function in government which looms larger than almost any other . . . It is the function which is normally carried out in private enterprise by the company secretary—that is the function of making sure that the firm has the proper legal and other authority to do whatever it is that it wishes to do . . . In government . . . this function is an extremely important one—so important that it has overshadowed all the rest. If you look through the volume of statutes for any recent year you will find that far and away the great majority of them are concerned with this sort of thing—the extension, modification and very occasionally the extinction of the powers of ministers and government departments. The reason for this is obvious enough; it is by holding these reins tightly—much more tightly than any body of shareholders holds the reins over a board of directors—that we secure in our democracy the political control over the activities of the executive. The outcome of a long series of political battles throughout our history has been that Parliament grants powers to ministers only when these are demonstrated to be necessary, only after political argument and debate, and usually with pretty severe and detailed limitations upon their exercise.'

Sir William may exaggerate the importance of Parliament and its debates in the present-day political scene. But the sheer weight of inherited definitions and limitations is a powerful negative force. While it is the excuse for Whitehall inertia, it is also the standing challenge to government to justify itself.

fication of self with too easily composed sets of verbalization? Can the definitions not be found in more straightforward notions of right and wrong which will provide both the shared assumptions to rally loyalties and the valid guides to action? Since the discrediting of some of the older ideologies, we have been increasingly summoned to action or to restraint by cries of 'moral' and 'immoral', 'good' and 'evil'. 'A moral attitude is not a policy', said Mr. Heath bravely enough in his Guildhall speech as he touched on the controversy over arms for South Africa. And admittedly the question of whether the British interest will be better served by supporting black savagery north of the Zambesi or white authoritarianism south of it can hardly be answered by a good-bad litmus test.

Nevertheless we feel uneasy if our governments are following policies which are not in accordance with our *mores*, with the body of daily custom by which we regulate our personal lives. And we regulate them not unsuccessfully. Can this not be extended? If we are to enjoy greater freedom for individual decision, which means the subordination of political advocacy to human ambition, then theoretically there is a case for a wider extension of moral judgement in public affairs. And if there is to be a new framework of law within which we are to enjoy great freedom, must this not mean laws which call rulers to account, and not laws to harass the subjects? Can we not apply the same criteria to our public and private acts?

V. Truth is Troth

V. Truth is Troth

If political debate and legal reasoning are anything to go by, a shared assumption of good and bad between rulers and ruled is the most unlikely eventuality. After two thousand years of European thought our moral philosophers are still arguing over definitions of 'goodness' and have been unable to demonstrate how any general code of ethics can be applicable to the general direction of the state. At best they doff their caps to 'good in common usage' or 'common-sense good' and return to the congenial schoolroom argument, fobbing off outsiders with the claim that the essence of the good is the continuing search for it.

Yet the ordinary run of men throughout the ages have had little difficulty in their daily doings in recognizing the good and discriminating between 'right' and 'wrong'. 'This is good', we confidently say of a fillet of fish, a musical performance, or an act of kindness, even though we ourselves may not always act in accordance with the recognition. Even under regimes which we have regarded as morally abhorrent, there was no great problem in 'common usage'. On taking over Italian secret police and Carabinieri files in 1941, I had expected —and even hoped for—some startling fresh insight into the nature of tyranny. What sort of sinister informers' reports, what confessions wrested under torture, what falsifications of fact would I uncover? But the contents might have been the routine reports of any village constable or any branch bank manager anywhere. The recurring phrase was *di buona condotta morale*. Was this praise for some unmentionable service?

Oh, no! explained the *maresciallo* in charge of records. It means that he is a good family man, that he has never been in trouble with the police, never in debt with shopkeepers. And turning the pages in the dossier, he pointed out: 'As you see, the bishop speaks well of him. So I could safely endorse his application for membership of the *partito*.' When the moment came to remove the officials of the *partito*, they were given sufficient time to deal with urgent duties in their offices, arrange for the payment of a widow's supplementary allowance, sort out emergency housing problems of refugees and the applications for admission to maternity wards. And having given instructions for the dispatch of rations to an orphans' home, they put down their telephones and announced dramatically: 'Signor Capitano, I am ready.'

Does this validate the notion—wrongly attributed to Machiavelli —that whatever the morality of princes, the subjects can continue to be good on their own terms? Not quite. If any 'good' Italian citizen had dared to shout 'Down with the Duce', an act which would not have been wrong in other countries, he would have been clapped inside by the *maresciallo*, his dependents would have received no supplementary allowances or rations and whichever person of *buona condotta morale* had denounced him would have been suitably rewarded. So the morality of princes does overshadow the good of common usage and break up the simple bonds of daily human relationships.

And in our time we have seen happenings in Europe for which only the adjective 'evil' is appropriate. Sooner or later this evil would have engulfed us all. The ordinary man had sensed this quickly enough while Fellows of All Souls, whom one would have considered the finest distillations of humane English academic essence, not only saw no evil in Naziism but were prepared to make a virtue out of surrendering free men to Hitler's thugs. The pre-war Conservative Party thereby rightly lost much of its credibility as a group capable of leading the nation.

The erosive effects of Vatican 'Machiavellianism' have also begun to show up. The ambiguous attitude of Pius XII in 1941 and 1942 towards the German–Italian campaign against Russia, and his refusal to support President Roosevelt's Lend-Lease for Russia may be excused in part as the agonies of a priest caught up in a conflict of which the outcome was uncertain. By the end of 1942 the Vatican excuses for ambiguity became less convincing. It is against this background of evasiveness that the Papacy must also be judged on whether at some stage it should have come out openly to prevent mass extermination. And just as the Cold War was beginning to freeze, the Vatican entered into an unholy alliance with the Italian Communist Party to prevent the introduction of civil divorce in Italy—an amoral miscalculation, as it turned out by 1970 when controversy over the same subject was threatening to disrupt Italian democracy. While the Italians' natural piety can be combined with scepticism over their priests, the consequences for clergy and laity in other lands have been corrosive: for in a changing world organized faiths must also display consistency. 'Your Majesty', said Pope Paul to Haile Selassie during the latter's official visit to the Vatican in November 1970, 'has shown how sensitive you are to the role of moral and spiritual values in a world in which brute force seems to threaten to overwhelm everything.'

A faith which is fighting a retreat—however prolonged—operates in a different moral setting from one which is still advancing, where errors of judgement will be excused and forgotten—if they were even noticed—in the common loyalty of the struggle. Knox could demand dogmatic adherence to his interpretations of the Scriptures while conceding the rights of subjects to rebel against temporal rule, preach the need for inward transformation of the individual but insist on strict obedience to the convenanted league. The inconsistencies were all subordinate to the goal of creating a national Protestant movement *vis-à-vis* a Catholic monarch, warring groups of barons, the intrigues of French power and the interventions of English court factions. The crude demagoguery of Knox was justified by the final establishment of a Scottish loyalty which had never hitherto existed: even if the resultant emotional unity emerged as self-righteous nationalism rather than as a new universal faith, the Scottish Reformation was relatively humane by the standards of the time and produced a comparatively tolerant society. Historically for the Scots the outcome was 'good' since it was better than what had gone before and proved the first step towards a wider British loyalty.

But when rulers and ruled are torn apart emotionally and loyalty and treachery have become meaningless notions, what sort of common good can rebind them? Any government, particularly a revolutionary one, which deliberately excludes from political participation sections of the people or marks them out for destruction, can hardly expect loyalty from them nor expect them to share its notions of what is good. Although this may have been clear enough with the first French Revolution and the Bolshevik Revolution, it was not so obvious as the *schleichendes Gift* spread in the years following the Nazi *Machtergreifung*. But by 1943 it was impossible for any German of normal sensitivity who was fully cognizant of what his government was doing at home and abroad to feel himself a traitor if he decided to work for the overthrow of Hitler. For the course of action on which the Nazis were by then embarked was the open and deliberate destruction of

H

everything which centuries of German lawmakers, thinkers, artists, nobles, and burghers had sought to create. Bonhoeffer could not be a traitor: betrayal was elsewhere. He was not of course unique: there were free-thinking and atheist socialists and others who did not flee and from the outset had not hesitated to oppose the Nazi regime and under torture perished unnoticed and unsung. At best this was rough historical justice since their part in destroying traditional German notions of good conduct and loyalty is thereby also forgotten.

In Austria after the 1918 Revolution, the emotional break was neither so decisive nor were the 'moral' issues so clear. The revolutionaries could never make up their minds as to what sort of Austria they hoped to create and who should be included or suppressed. The Social-Democrats were never quite successful in making Dollfuss appear a villain. The moral issues are even less clear with the Greeks who for more than half a century have gone through an irregular but still distinctive cycle of parliamentarianism, near-anarchy, government by royal decree, military dictatorship, royal restoration, and recommencement of the cycle. The 'Outs' generally move to comfortable exile in London or Paris to become the darlings of the Philhellenes and wait for their turn to come round again, while the same secret police continue to apply the same brutal treatment to what looks like a standing list of suspects. A contemporary Briton, Dutchman, or Scandinavian may legitimately find the process distasteful but he is not justified in singling out any one phase as evil nor in idealizing those who lost the last round. Moral as well as historical perspective is certainly lost when the Council of Europe proceeds to expel the Greeks for detaining a bouzouki player while happily continuing to accept the Turks who murdered their former head of government under rather nasty circumstances.

The strands of history are still too separate for any one thread of good or evil to be stretched across frontiers except in circumstances such as Nazi Germany, Stalin's Russia, and Haile Selassie's Ethiopia. Although the last two find their defenders in the West, it is easier to make out a case for Governor Eyre of Jamaica, whose brutal suppression of the negro uprising in 1865 at least saved the island from the continuing miseries of Haiti and gave it a hundred years of relative peace and welfare. He was not without some humanitarian motives, as his contemporaries did admit, while none can possibly be ascribed to either Stalin or Haile Selassie: their concern was and is with power.

What will be the moral judgement on the Nazi era a hundred

years from now? Some negative benefits such as the destruction of the military cult will be noted. Professor Ralf Dahrendorf sees the Nazis as the main instrument in the creation of liberal modernity in Germany since they effectively destroyed the older authoritarianism: undoubtedly 'good Germans' such as those who offered the only major act of resistance to Hitler would have restored something like older German notions of virtue and élitism. But this might have prevented the growth of the present working compromise between German respect for law and the extension of individual freedom of choice. Morality and liberalism which had parted company have now been brought together again in a way which painstaking constitutional models such as the Weimar Constitution could never effect. But this is merely to argue in Hegelian terms the portentous power of the negative, not to pass judgement.

In a long enough perspective the Nazis may appear to be beyond good and evil and merely a link in some chain of necessities. Nevertheless the majority of Western European peoples, including Germans and Austrians, will in our time still continue to regard them as evil. From this two consequences can be drawn. First, a moral decision or issue in politics is a contemporary affair, and second it is impossible to sustain hypocrisy all the way down to the lowest and broadest strata of society. Rulers may sustain it among themselves, philosophers may justify 'saving lies' and dissemblance as essential to the daily lubrication of human relations, while at the other extreme it has been the fatal mistake of liberal intellectuals, such as Ernst Niekisch, to indulge in negative criticism of our present state and propagate perfectionist schemes impossible for normal human beings to implement. But for the broad mass of the people the good does mean something in daily usage: they could not live without some daily dependable notion of it.

From which it would appear that good and evil are essentially *intuitive* notions of concern to *living* men. And if society is not plunged into complete moral chaos it is thanks to our sense of the continuity of human life in society. This enables us to cope with the paradox of unintended consequences resulting from any simple appeal to goodness—when the best intentions bring evil results and good consequences often flow from evil acts. Unlike the schoolman struggling with verbal propositions, for the commonalty a concept is the history of the concept and this applies to the concept of goodness as to any other. In trying to satisfy the impulses which govern our lives, we take up what is the received notion of what is good and by a combination of intuition and post-facto rationalization try to evolve our individual applications. Self-interest of some individuals or groups may blind them to factors apparent to others, but in every organized European society there is some common basis of custom, institutions, and sufficient objects of utility or delight for a common factor of good to be identifiable by the majority. Strictly speaking, a homogeneous society with common assumptions created by a common history should not require a great deal more. Such faithful adherence may be strengthened by the belief of subjects that their ruler or leader is a 'good living' man but equally so can the belief that he possesses to an exaggerated degree the more human failings of his subjects: both attributes appear to endow him with virtue.

If 'human values' are thus rarely in doubt for the individual in a distinctively human situation, it can only be because they were well established in advance of verbal definition and possibly even before coherent language had developed. It is only when human relationships are denied or distorted that 'values' disappear or enjoy currency in some perverted form. What is remarkable is their consistency in spite of changes in intellectual fashion, in forms of government, or theological absolutism. This has been so obvious and sensed for so long that our blindness in this respect is perhaps the phenomenon to be studied and not our moral sense itself. Least of all can Christians lay special claim; as Buckle stated: '. . . to assert that Christianity communicated to men moral truths previously unknown, argues on the part of the assertor, either gross ignorance or wilful fraud'.

The Egyptian Book of the Dead, the Babylonian Hymn to Samas, the Analects of Confucius, Plato, the Mosaic law, Norse texts, and the rules of the Redskin camp all bear this out.[1] Duties within the family, the virtues of courage and of protecting the weak, the precepts of honesty over contracts and property are all present in those societies, as one might expect from 'values' whose origins are in the biology of human life and in the ways of hunters, herdsmen, and cultivators. But we find too that the Golden Rule and what our churchmen proudly hail as the distinctive contribution of Christianity emerge among somewhat unexpected surroundings and peoples. 'He who loves his

---

[1] A convenient short comparative list of the rules of ancient wisdom is to be found as an Appendix to *The Abolition of Man* by the late C. S. Lewis (Riddell Memorial Lectures, Bles, 1946).

life loses it', Christ is reputed to have said. But the Norseman writes in the Hamaval: 'I hung on the gallows for nine nights wounded with the spear as a sacrifice to Odin, myself offered to Myself.' And the two pagan warrior peoples, Romans and Norsemen, had anticipated the later humanists. 'Men were brought into existence for the sake of men that they might do one another good', wrote Cicero, to which the Norse bard replies: 'Man is man's delight.'

Such precepts were doubtless observed in those far-off societies in much the same proportion as they are to-day. If our moral philosophers had devoted their energies to establishing why and on what occasions they were not observed instead of arguing over what absolute and universal imperative would ensure their observance, they might have by now answered some of our political ethical questions. Negative evidence can be revealing. For it is easy to see why the rules should be obeyed: they are those which will foster distinctively human qualities.

What are they—these human qualities which intuition and the primitive inheritance of wisdom first sensed and later formulated? They are the conscious extension of our natural instincts and capacities: and the capacity may be even more important than the instinct. The expectations of the child nourished under the care of its parents evolve into hope which remains with most of us throughout our lives. Dependence becomes conscious trust in others while desire consciously grasped emerges as will; and in the period of childhood play which even the simplest society in the human species permits its young, the child creates for himself conscious purpose which will take its adult form from initiation and custom. Finally comes the capacity to acquire skill by conscious learning, the precious human possession which gave us mastery of our environment and opportunities for individual assertion of a non-animal kind. The herd instinct in its conscious shaping as loyalty or fidelity, and the mating impulse which gives and receives affection and protects and trains the young, have developed as conscious altruism and point to the conscious precept of self-sacrifice.

Absence of these qualities or capacities meant the disappearance of family and tribe, their full possession brought the greatest advancement to the group, its victory in battle, and the secure enjoyment of the fruits of victory. If they also allow for compromise, magnanimity, and forgiveness this should not surprise us since they are attributes to be found in all known societies to-day, although the extent and manner in which they may be exercised cannot be equated between groups. Their evolution in society has been fostered at least as much by exclusivity as by extension. In his Romanes Lecture of 1943, Sir Julian Huxley found us suffering from the primitive difficulties of 'individual moral adjustment' and from some primitive 'super-ego'. At an early stage mankind made an excellent adjustment in the moral field: it merely became conscious of what it had been doing instinctively and primitive societies show no sign of a super-ego— rather the contrary.

The human qualities themselves determined the evolution of moral consciousness. They can be present in peace and war, slavery or in freedom, in all manner of social situation. The first *moral* conflicts may have arisen when men had to decide what was the appropriate attribute in some specific situation and such primitive Cornelian tragedies were played out before men had language to describe them, since their first artefacts lie among fragments of jaw which could not have uttered the words of any known language. And when words first became adequate to describe them, this was certainly in the form of verbs (to hope, to trust, and to try) rather than as nouns. For they were directed towards an end by impulses such as hunger, greed, fear, or sex—drives which were still stronger than the slowly disengaging consciousness of self. A general notion of 'goodness' could only come late in the day when men had relaxed sufficiently to be able to isolate their attributes mentally and endow them with some absolute attribute in a specific context of desire, and by the rites and fairy tales of magical animism represent their own qualities in crude symbolic form as virtues. God could be good and the *seigneur* be *débonnaire*—provided the homonyms were available.

And as killing became the craft and livelihood of mankind it accelerated the growth of a distinctly disengaged consciousness of self. At the end of the half-million years of transition through jackal to true predator, men were sufficiently detached from the natural process to sense it as a conflict of life and death in which they were both actors and spectators. For most of the time they were avid cannibals from necessity or fury, but in the end they had to organize even their cannibalism in order not to disrupt family and tribal life completely. As the transition neared its end, the dead were no longer eaten but buried with some evidence of ceremony. Looking at the corpses of his kith and kin, primitive insight whispered: This is you! Cain had recognized Abel. And with this consciousness of self comes the sense that there is a relationship other than what is found in the appearances. Men could turn inwards.

Our attitudes towards our own human attributes must of necessity be emotive, expressive, and persuasive, to use A. J. Ayer's well-worn phrase, since it is through them that we retain our essential links with survival and that insight enables us to recognize the same motives in others. The need to acquire and possess underlies the process: 'ought' came before 'is' which represents a later stage of self-conscious identity. If the Lowland Scot stands by the letter of obligation to an exaggerated degree, in his tongue 'ought' still retains its original power of possession. Some peoples of the earth have not yet even acquired a verb 'to be' although they are not less moral for its absence.

And even to-day, overtones of the magic world are associated with virtues as well as with their opposites in the conflict of life and death —those qualities of despairing, doubting, fearing, and betraying—all that we sense as destructive of a man's identity. And when only these destructive qualities are present then we have evil—the state of no humanity. Rulers who base their power solely on the exploitation of the destructive qualities can be justly stigmatized while those who treat men only as objects or intellectual abstractions may find themselves on the same slippery slope. After some half-million years or so it is not to be wondered that in human predicaments some intuitive notion of what is 'good' should break into our consciousness and that we can believe in a conscience. And since witchcraft always lingers on for longer than the belief in good spirits, the frequency with which the word 'evil' appears in *The Times* newspaper or the *Guardian* indicates that editors are affected as much as those obscure and troubled persons who sneak into country churches to turn candles upside down.

The need for moral decisions over the whole of society thus remains. In considering the survival needs of the group, authority must be exercised so as to keep the human qualities in balance. This particularly applies in problems where the element of individual feeling is dominant and where group objectives are ill-defined. On one side we see the extension of gentler ways in daily life and a spread of superficial philanthropic sentiments, and on the other an alarming growth of mass cruelty and the indiscriminate denunciation of men as categories, while the dehumanization of our institutions is leading to marked outbreaks of animal violence. Irrational racial doctrines in one generation lead in the next to a maudlin preoccupation with

other races to such an extent that we find virtue in committing treachery against our own kind—the ultimate evil as far as there is one in
human terms. And when we finally reach the stage where our political
concepts are all in doubt at one and the same time and where our
sense of identity is weakened, some form of moral restatement is
essential.

For in the contemporary British political world it is at times
impossible to make oneself heard above the clamour of politicians
shouting each other down as immoral, when it is plain that the qualities
they have in common are selfishness, vanity, ignorance and stupidity.
The invocation of some universal principle such as Love has as much
relevance as invoking X or Y. For love involves quarrels, jealousies,
self-torture, and the infliction of pain on others. Love is no more
perpetual benevolence than any other human attribute and does not
become so by latinizing it as Charity.

How do we clear away the undergrowth and find a fresh path? If
in some way all the citizenry could have direct experience of or participation in political decision, the human intuitions might be enough.
In some contemporary societies the atmosphere and circumstances
may be particularly conducive for human qualities to be taken into
account when political decisions are pending. If a country's laws
have been directed mainly towards the support and encouragement
of family life, the sense of obligation which has had its main intuitive
development within the family will be more readily extended to
other members of society. Our sense of community is still largely a
family one and the grown man's tendency to look back on childhood
and upbringing and see them in a roseate hue is the emotional basis
for most of our religious, moral, political, and other attachments.
Many of the apprehensions over 'youth' prove groundless when the
former teenager and his girl-friend marry and find that traditional
notions of authority and morality are useful adjuncts in bringing up
a family. Self-expression stops short at having the porridge thrown
round the room at breakfast time.

Where pressures are destructive of the family, this basis of society
is undermined. So far the family has undergone fringe changes in
accordance with other fashions of the times: but it still survives.
Soviet Russia tried to abolish it and failed. Progressive Anglican clerics
are making a more dangerous and subtle attempt by encouraging
the break-up of the homogeneity from which the family pattern derives. But if family morality was part of the starting point of the

ethical process, it is certainly not the end. If under Naziism it provided the main refuge into which German decency withdrew, the field of political decision was left clear for Hitler and Himmler. The Russians live their warm-hearted personal lives independently of the morality —such as it is—of their governmental system, but this does not save them from the domination of an inhuman code in their public life.

The difficulty is that while we can spot when certain regimes such as that of Hitler have launched themselves on the path of destruction, we have not throughout history been able to identify any particular political system as possessing some special ethical quality. Governments have historically fulfilled a number of roles. They have been concerned with the consolidation of central power, as with Louis XIV of France; they have promoted a particular design of society, such as was conceived by Frederick the Great or by Bismarck; they have been mainly occupied with reconciling conflicting interests or peoples, as with mediæval Poland, the Austro-Hungarian Empire, present-day European democracies, and tribal-sectarian oligarchies such as the Lebanon. The toleration of separate competing interests is not a special virtue of liberal parliamentarianism, and there have been as many ways of producing reconciliations over the common good as there have been forms of government. Initially not even the Nazis willed the bad, and every age has noted that contemporaries who have striven most valiantly to establish moral imperatives are liable to make a choice of evil *sub specie beni*. If there is a dialectical case for an objective good, the present processes of human thinking do not appear to demonstrate how to arrive at it. This is not to justify whatever is, *à la* E. H. Carr, but to learn to withhold moral condemnation from political forms which do not reflect our favoured self-image.

At most one can say that the greater the degree of accountability of the rulers, the more likely is the political system to encourage moral actions among those carrying the greatest responsibilities. Such an authority may suffer from human weakness and selfishness but will also profit from human strength and generosity and where its laws appear to be based on common assumptions—either intuitive or rational—they will be accepted as impartial. Authority can be more than impartial: it will be purposeful if the active members of society feel that their own purposes are identified with those in authority. But a power wielder as such can only make a purely moral decision when he is in the fortunate position of being able to consider a problem of government solely in his own human terms. If he has to consider the interests of other human beings, then an element of calculation enters and he must make his decisions in terms of 'better' or 'worse', which are concepts of expediency. The calculation is generally between a number of courses of action, any or all of which may result in some inhumanity to man. If we decide for reasons of expediency that inhuman consequences are the lesser evil, as in the case of the Punjab at the time of Indian independence, the outcome can hardly be said to be moral but neither is it immoral.

And as a test whether there is a generally acceptable ethical framework of human purpose, one need only note each time the word 'moral' appears in political usage and consider whether it has contributed anything of substance to the argument. It generally turns out to be a piece of emphatic tautology introduced to intimidate opponents, in accordance with the McCarthyite smear technique now in vogue in the Anglo-Saxon and Nordic world among Liberal and Left-Wing circles who find that their dogma no longer stand up to rational analysis. 'Browbeating and kow-towing are not words in the vocabulary of moral obligation,' says H. J. Blackham:[2] but they are certainly common usage among twentieth-century moralists. 'Moral responsibility' is a phrase much in political vogue but the morality is inherent in the responsibility: it is analogous to the notorious Americanism 'meaningful' often used to try to give conviction to a meaningless utterance.

Does the issue of cruelty not provide a firmer foundation for a moral dialectic in politics? Religion offers no guidance and up to two hundred years ago while torture was still part of the judicial process in the more 'Christian' states, the priest stood by to provide 'spiritual' comfort to the tortured. History can only tell us that growing security enables us to be more humane.[3] The first requirement of

---

[2] *Political Discipline In A Free Society* (Allen and Unwin, 1961), p. 191.

[3] Nature provides even less guidance. Sherrington could only note that suffering increased in proportion as lives ascend life's scale. His judgement on the recurring human situation was: 'Hume's dialogue puts the question whether the pain of the world is or is not offset by its joy . . . One thing we can discern as a factor in this question. At least it is a harmony . . . That we should have attained that knowledge is an inexpressibly estimable good. It is, so far as we detect, uniquely, the possession of ourselves—it is *the* human possession.' Sir C. Sherrington, *Man on His Nature* (C.U.P., 1951), p. 291. Men have an infinite capacity for suffering, for indulgence, for finding satisfaction in everything including martyrdom.

a ruler is thus the creation of conditions where men will feel secure and not be subject to arbitrariness: in fulfilment of this he can no doubt justify the infliction of pain on others. But he stands condemned if he encourages or knowingly tolerates arbitrary brutality by his officers of state, and in such a case our intuition will be on the side of subjects who seize the first favourable opportunity to pay back in kind. In our wartime encouragement of resistance against Naziism, we stretched the laws of war to vanishing point. In our post-war era both civil and military courts, while condemning barbarity against those entitled to the protection of law, have rightly taken into consideration the human reactions of soldiers and police called upon to combat terrorism. The urgency with which Stalin's successors proclaimed a return to 'Socialist legality' showed a sound calculation of the danger to the Soviet system which his arbitrary cruelty had represented.

The use of torture in France and by French security forces during the Algerian terrorist campaign was denounced as a cancer of democracy, implying that it could be excised from the French system by exposure and rigorous judicial action. Regrettably it is nothing of the sort. From wartime liaison with French security services I was to find that such methods are an established practice in the whole police system and part of an unbroken tradition leading back to pre-Revolution days. The nominal abolition of torture by the Revolution was hardly reflected in Jacobin practice. French indignation and protests against the Algerian tortures were largely confined to a few intellectuals and students and aroused little popular response. The French are a callous people.

And historical judgements on cruelty are present-day reactions. The mediæval portraits of hangmen and torturers show that cruelty was recognized and hated as such. But other emotions were involved to a different degree so that we run the risk of attributing our self-conscious attitudes to less self-conscious historical participants. The dilemmas where men do strange things under external pressures, such as battlefield experiences, are probably more akin to the situations which confronted Europeans in the Middle Ages. No one emotional element can ever be separated from the total reactions of human beings of any one age and singled out for moral condemnation or approval. Otherwise we are faced by the sterile question of how to order rationally our intuitive reactions in an objective hierarchy of values, and quite a few philosophic reputations have been shattered in the attempt. In practice what results is a spectrum of emotional colourings evoked by the words 'good' or 'moral'. The higher good is usually only realizable over the corpses of those whose lesser goods thwart our own aspirations. The sponsorship of African terrorism by a number of our churchmen is only the most recent case.

The excuse which can be made for the clerical ranters is that once again they have committed the error of treating their emotional reactions to a decision or event as part of the substance of the decision itself. Forgetting that the perception is the cause of the anger and that the anger is not the cause of the perception we turn the Golden Rule into orgies of self-righteousness. Self-consciousness does of course create a heightened sense of individual commitment, so that Kant without any hypocrisy could produce his dictum that an act is moral if, and only if, we wish that it should become a universal law. But latter-day manifestations of this doctrine suggest that it makes us less lenient with others than with ourselves.

And in the meantime too great a theological and political investment has gone into the claim that there can be objectivity in moral values. It is an easy way of mustering irrational forces against political opponents. Those who consciously or subconsciously realize that they are inadequately equipped as human beings, seek protective colouring by invoking moral censure on those who might show up their inadequacy, and even seek to justify their own shortcomings by trying to pass off their lack of human qualities as the qualities themselves. Humanitarianism is invoked as camouflage for their own fears: cowardice masquerades as morality: hate for X is passed off as love for Y. So the faces of those doing something from duty begin to bear the mark of the Cain they are denouncing. Here is an 'ought' deriving from deprivation not possession. The intuition of others who are not so affected senses the falsehood and protests, often crudely. To a surprising and gratifying degree British electorates have seen through much of this cant because they have sensed the element of reversion in it.

When we turn from *a priori* argument and examine a major issue in its historical setting, moral clarification in politics becomes less complicated. The greatest moral issue of recent centuries, namely slavery, was resolved not because of general ethical agreement but because our heightened self-consciousness made it impossible for us to impose or maintain in a servile status human beings to whom we attributed our own sensitivity. But this was not linked to any institutionalized set of political ideas. Over the same period the Emperor Josef II emancipated the serfs in the face of the opposition of the

Austrian nobility and the Hungarian magnates. While Napoleon I drove his soldiers into carnage, he abolished slavery and accorded civic status to Jews as his armies advanced. As far as official moralities had been concerned, slavery had always been provided with excellent justification from the Greeks through St Thomas Aquinas to the Renaissance Popes who imposed the ban of slavery on cities and states which defied their spiritual authority. The problems which the contemporary world has inherited from slavery, mostly in the New World, require from our own generation not special agonies of conscience but the practical solutions which good government in the European style can generally produce.

It is not however so easy to get rid of an ethical colouring once acquired. For once in our consciousness, any object or problem is caught up in the Western conceptualizing process. Because morality has been increasingly a matter for conceptual formulation in European thought, it has acquired the appearance of evolving in the direction of greater rationality. But there is still no special category of ethical reasoning: attempts to prove the existence of higher values merely illustrate that given certain verbal assumptions such as higher and lower, one can draw certain verbal conclusions about them. In ethical discussion, 'metaphysical', 'subjective', 'spiritual', and 'emotional' have become interchangeable, and 'truth' which in its human context once meant 'troth' or *Treue* finds itself subordinated to 'verification' for non-human ends. At times we find it impossible to recognize in the words what we feel in our hearts. So far we have coped with the resultant errors largely because of the acceptance in daily usage of the shared European inheritance of custom. There is only the one basic conceptual relationship, that between subject and object as it has been evolving in its specifically Western context.

And power itself does not become moral or immoral as a result of the constitutional setting. What corrupts is not the power but the circumstances which hedge about a king and may cut him off from normal human relations, so that his thoughts are not subject to the sort of cross-checking against daily realities and other people's arguments. The British Cabinet practice, by which a Prime Minister's official advisers in attendance may not challenge him but only answer his questions, was a major element in policy errors, such as Suez, which were later condemned in moral terms. The men involved were all moral enough, but a governmental process which does not challenge a man to show his human qualities is an a-moral one.

But if there is no separate category of political morality to which authority can be subordinated, are the subjects not exposed to special risks if their loyalty is unquestioned? Although trying to be good men and ready to shoulder their share of responsibility, are they not liable to be caught up in some general criminal purpose? 'I always told the Duce the truth,' wept Commendatore Menapace, head of the O.V.R.A.[4] in Italian East Africa as I led him away. 'I did more than my duty,' exclaimed General Mambrini, the Commander of the Italian African Police as I similarly removed him—Italian anti-Fascists were highly amused by this remark. A German who had always done what he believed to be right and had *Gott Mit Uns* embossed on his belt buckle, finds himself in a firing squad shooting *francs tireurs*: is it right in turn that after defeat he may be deprived of civic privilege and even shot himself? This could happen to any of us. The answer is doubtless that it is not right, that leaders will make errors, and their followers will have to pay for them and this is one of the lessons of history. For the individual this means that he can refuse to accept acts of government as having in themselves any moral quality and treat his rulers as capable of making the same errors as himself.

The theoretical advantage of systems of popular representation is not that they are more moral than other forms of government nor that they develop a higher ethical sense in their leaders (there is a case for showing that they may do the opposite in that they enable responsibility to be too easily shuffled off) but that so far in European history they have permitted the widest range of opportunities to counter human errors by the governing elements. If they fail to do this as the parliamentary system failed to do in France, the case for introducing another system becomes overwhelming. Latter-day liberals, still trying to present human progress as an emancipation and in the form of an opposition between morality and power, have largely lost influence because they were readier to find evil in authoritarian systems than offer practical means of countering error in representational ones.

Professor Lionel Trilling, one of the Liberal exponents, finds that there is dishonesty and hypocrisy when the Liberal takes office and throws over his scruples.[5] If there was dishonesty at all, it was in

[4] The department of the Fascist Ministry of the Interior concerned with the suppression of anti-Fascist activity.
[5] *The Liberal Imagination* (Mercury Books, 1961).

the mind of the Liberal at the beginning when he advanced a creed which he must have known would be irrelevant in the business of administering the community. In fact it has been less a question of dishonesty than of intellectual confusion. Morality having become a concept is concerned with rational definition while power is experience and application. And when we begin to discover evil consequences as the result of the acts of good men and refuse to accept that good things may be happening in societies run by evil men, we are applying the wrong concept: the test should not have been 'good' or 'evil'. We are thus disappointed when Franco fails to collapse and Africans not only appear to be prospering under *apartheid* but happily emigrate from emancipated African territories to share in its material benefits. Liberalism suffers some moral hurt in such situations so that its followers begin to behave in an illiberal way to the discredit of their creed. Liberalism to-day is essentially an intellectual approach to politics and the one thing it will find mortal is intellectual dishonesty.

The liberal may try to get round this by claiming that his motives are pure while those of Franco and Vorster are impure. This position is only defensible while he abstains from action. The moment he acts, the intellectualizations he was pleased to call liberal values are submitted to the test of human relationships and actions. Human attributes at that point become more important than abstractions about human motivation. From the safe distance of Westminster Gladstone could describe the bombardment of Alexandria as 'this solemn act' while the United Nations claimed the best of motives for their troops murdering, looting, and raping in the Congo. Men can only be discussed as ends in themselves or in terms of concepts of value when they are not involved as instrumentalists or as instruments, and this does not happen in daily life. All the liberal humanist can do is to make allowance for human error, and it is one of the signs of liberal bankruptcy that he no longer dares to do so.

Alas! As one of liberal descent and inclination, I wonder why he seems to go even further and delves back into the past to relieve himself of feelings of guilt by ascribing innocence to others. In this sort of moral orgy our ex-colonies are favourite objects. Hardly a week passes without B.B.C. Programme Three featuring an Oxbridge female don or lady novelist who in a high tense voice describes her discovery that there is no piped water in M'bongoland or that there is a high percentage of illiteracy in some community where once the Union Jack fluttered. The Imperial era is presented as one of neglect and exploitation and we are invited to don sackcloth and ashes and fork out cash. In daily practice 'imperialism' consisted of patient and usually disheartening efforts by district officers to persuade one village to construct a reservoir and lay down a water main, or another to build a schoolhouse to receive an expensively trained teacher provided free of charge. If the official had tried any other method except patient persuasion, there would have been loud howls in the House of Commons from the tense ladies' political boy-friends. Since there is not the slightest evidence that our former colonial subjects will permit our moral notions to be imposed on them, nor indeed will they permit morality in any sense that we conceive it to become a constituent element in their relationship with us, the tense ladies can only be regarded as the last nervous twitchings of an already dead imperial eagle. In this situation feelings of guilt or innocence are irrelevant.

When we reach this stage where our concepts are upside-down and are letting *us* down, and we are faced by the paradox of unintended consequences, it is neither malign fate nor punishment for our guilt. It means that we have hung on for too long to out-of-date verbalizations and that truth requires a new formulation. We are apparently passing through a period analogous to the thirteenth century when there was a major shift in the human order, when feudal notions began to acquire a specialist and even pejorative connotation, and when the *wizhid* of A.D. 1200 in its sense of practical knowing shifted to being the higher-order principle of 1300 and was invoked as the abstraction of knowledge. In spite of the later periodic emergence of really cunning ones like Lloyd George, *Kunst* no longer automatically ensured *Gunst*. At the same time the new order of ruling princes, merchant cities, and trained *Landsknecht* formations had not yet conceptualized its own vocabulary of description. It even took three hundred years for Grotius and Puffendorf to tidy up the old out-of-date descriptions into a code of sorts.

In such periods traditional assumptions get in the way of rational thinking. Intuition has to fill the gap, spluttering somewhat incoherently for lack of an adequate conceptual order, as no doubt the retired district officers do when they switch off the tense female broadcasters. Our persistence in stretching the vocabulary of rationalizing morality into fields where it can never be applicable, instead of restricting it to its proper role of definition of intuitive moral relationships, distorts the whole motivation of action. Most of all do we suffer from the domination of one-time rational notions in the field of economic affairs, where forms of greed which would have been restrained by tradition have entrenched themselves so strongly that reason has not been able to dislodge them with factual evidence. So wilder forms of emotional argument are summoned up as correction and decked out in rationalizing guise. European civilization to-day stands in greatest danger from outwardly rational frameworks such as Christianity, Marxism, and Naziism, careering off on their own. For in such cases human beings will be treated as objects and untruth threatens.

If the consequences could be confined to professors, journalists, and professional parliamentarians, we should not worry overmuch. Unfortunately the consequences have brought trial and humiliation to the British people as a whole, who are too intimidated to retort as they see their streets turned into multi-racial sewers in the name of human dignity; and as they struggle with the resultant personal and family predicaments they are told that their faithful adherence has become prejudice rendering them liable to fines and legal charges based on a denunciation by Mark Bonham-Carter. If they show the normal healthy reaction against scroungers and wrong-doers, then 'equality' or 'compassion' is thrown back in their faces with a moral parsley surround. All they can sense is a feeling of let-down and betrayal. And in this they are justified. For in its origins 'morality' was essentially the restraint of the individual in deference to the needs of the group, while now there is compulsory concession to individual indulgence. So the man in the street senses that good and bad have somehow been stood on their heads. A notion of good should bind people —as the word *religio* implies. It should not separate them. The good ought to mean loyalty.

Meanwhile the religious moralist has landed in a state of complete confusion. The bases of the moral-intellectual authority of Western Christianity crumbled when we ceased to regard 'Man' as a separate creation. While the simple-minded have gone on accepting the objects of reverence offered by the churches and a fair number of the more sophisticated have seen the desirability of society possessing objects of reverence, the church leaders themselves have resorted increasingly to threats against those who ignore or challenge their authority. Their theological substantiations prove to be only good in parts since the authority of, say, St. Augustine or St. Thomas Aquinas must stand or fall on a complete doctrine: if this is only palatable in portions then the divine authority requires qualification. No faggots in front

I

of the Escorial nor stakes in the Solway Firth will restore the absolutism of Theodore of Mopsuestia or that of the Anglican Articles.

Western Christianity, suffering from the same inversion created by our self-consciousness, has everywhere degenerated into self-righteousness and the divine image has become defiled by the same process which has besmirched Man. Protestant churches display the same lack of compassion which characterized the Anglican-Evangelical attitude to the Irish potato famine, while declaring themselves doughty champions of distant causes of emancipation and conversion. The symptoms of behaviour towards each new version of the infidel from the First Crusade to our own time and through the entire process of extroversion, conversion, and inversion show little change, and the jackal mask once worn by primitive shamans is very visible on our clergy. 'Oh, for a closer walk with God,' sang the psalmist and '*dona nobis pacem*' rumble the tympani in Beethoven's *Missa Solemnis*. But these are just what the one-time shepherds are so anxious to deny to the flocks who still look to them for the rites which sustain their human attributes in daily suffering, joy, sacrifice, and fulfilment. Ecclesiastical support for schemes of material change or for scapegoat hunts where power is the aim and expediency the method, cannot satisfy such emotional needs.

The final bankruptcy of religious insight comes with the modernist Roman Catholic view that: 'Failure alone . . . is due to the creature while success is due to God. Choice is possible because the creature's desire for the greater good may conflict with his desire for the lesser good. Hence if he allows his attention to focus on the lesser but more immediate good, he falls, and the cause lies in himself. God allows the creature to have a negative priority over his own act of causality: God modifies his causality in accordance with the creature's failure. This does not mean that the creature is outside God's control in any contradictory sense since God sees and permits from eternity for the sake of the ultimate good.'[6]

If we are therefore to assume that there is some divine purpose behind the mass suffering of our century, it is one which human beings whose lives have to be lived in a natural span have a right to reject. It is no part of our end and aim to glorify such gods. In our naïve days we may have been prepared to accept the massacre of

[6] *Prospect For Metaphysics*, ed. Ian T. Ramsey. Essay by Mark Pontifex of Downside Abbey (Allen and Unwin, 1961), p. 136.

innocents, but we can no more stomach this now than we can slavery and torture. So one great gain which may result from our heightened self-consciousness may be at long last the recognition that our values are to be found in our own attributes and not in some higher-order explanation.

The moral problem in politics turns out to be not one of imperatives, rationalization, or institutionalized ethics but of ensuring that men retain their totality of human qualities in pursuit of their aims. The danger to society arises not from the origins of these aims in brutish desires since these can be countered by other human attributes, but because ideas and institutions can dehumanize us, whatever the imperative invoked. Evil as the arbitrary treatment of other human beings can masquerade under a thousand seductive disguises, even humanist ones. For although men can find the springs of right action in their own nature, if we replace this nature by a theoretical 'Man' we risk a more blind and arrogant dogmatism than could have been devised even by the late mediæval church: the latter still had some doubts about the nature of god and his purpose. 'Man' has no doubts and now seems to be demanding human sacrifice, preferably white and Rhodesian, and looks like landing us in the same predicament as Pope Paul sacrificing the inmates of Auschwitz, Dachau and Buchenwald for the sake of the secular survival of the institution.

Need we be trapped in this spiral of betrayal? The trouble originates in a combination of over-proccupation with self and with monolithic ideas. We cannot suddenly reverse the former since it is inherent in human evolution: but the second can be tackled. It is through a pluralism of ideas and of authorities that we shall find release and end the tyranny of God, Man, Morality, Freedom, with their capital G, M, and F. It would almost be a matter for rejoicing if there were some foundation for ecclesiastical condemnations of 'neo-paganism'. For in their pantheon the classical pagans deified all recognizable human attributes and at least came to terms with some of the less recognizable without necessarily admitting them as gods. This nice compromise of instinct and imagery still determines our daily deeds more than we like to admit. There are days when we feel mercurial, some when we are martial, occasions which call for a pinch of incense to Pallas Athene and others for a prayer to Venus. Since we cannot return to pure intuition nor revive the Greek pantheon, we have to support our human insights on contemporary occasions by a reasoned assessment of the appropriateness of one human quality rather than another. This is *moral* discrimination and one which each individual can make for himself.

It is the misdirection of human qualities by ideas rather than the qualities themselves which present the danger. Even those attributes which in our catechisms and lecture-room ethics are treated as least edifying have proved less pernicious to human societies than ideologies. Greed and aggression are outward-looking so that even the human need for more effective weapons of mastery has helped in the greatest advances of human welfare. The so-called universal values on the other hand have been responsible both for indiscriminate suffusing of emotion and doom-laden inversion. The present blockage of the process by which the Western world has in the past thrown up new ideas results from an inability to free our consciousness from the monolithic concepts on which we believe our identity to be dependent. Since in the course of European history the inter-play between subject and object has in our minds been conceived through analogies of opposites—Freedom and Authority, Good and Evil, Mind and Matter—this inability may derive from an anxiety lest the inimical or negative opposing factor may overwhelm us. Deliver us from evil, we pray, as we commit it!

So although men sense simple notions of good and bad among each other and these still bind them together, they are not enough as guides to the actions of an authority seeking to rally loyalty. The Western objectifying consciousness requires a wider formulation of coherent ideas. If Man cannot provide this, can men not do so? Must there only be one road of virtue? If the universal seems to produce falsehood, can the particular not provide truth? For men's troth can only hold in terms of what they know to be true towards one another.

VI. Identities from the Past

VI. Identities from the Past

At the root of our trouble is an inability to find some vantage point from which we can truly look upon ourselves as objects. A process of definition of Man which cannot go beyond the subject to be defined was bound to come up against this snag. This is even made a virtue. 'It is impossible to judge an event from outside. It is at the heart of the absurd misfortune that one keeps the right to despise it', wrote Albert Camus in his *Cahiers*. We thus arrive at a view of existence where everything is contingency or where everything is necessity. Sooner or later this leads us to treating our internal spasms as intimations of impending revelation.

An alternative metaphysical justification is offered us by Professor Voegelin. 'Creations of empire have always had claim to representative humanity,' he says, and the conquerors 'were consciously aware of the affinity of meaning between their conquests and the spiritual efflorescence of representative humanity'.[1] There is of course no such transcendent *Schlachtduft*. Voegelin offers only another example of a European projecting his need for authority on to some image which will give him an illusion of identity. This has existed since our earliest historical chapter. Alexander wept because he thought he had come to the end of his conquests: but he still carried on after his death as the rider and horse which gave the stamp of authenticity to the tribal coinages of pre-Roman Europe. Our present search for an orderly world has been bedevilled by the continual recasting of such images derived from old gods, heroes, and emperors. The assumption that order must exist under some supreme authority is so unquestionably accepted that we cannot conceive of an empire that is not holy and Roman although no empire has ever been both. The universal loyalty becomes the betrayal of the particular, as with our latest attempt to realize a world *impero* through the United Nations. If this is 'a global

[1] Stevenson Memorial Lecture. Royal Institute of International Affairs, 1962.

ecumene in search of a world', to quote Professor Voegelin again, it does seem to involve taking sides against our brothers.

The freezing of all human motives and attributes into a universal category labelled Man thus appears to result in great part from failure to make a fresh distinction between first- and second-order factors in human affairs, between general and particular causes. The European ability to do this has been the continuous red thread running through the growth and elaboration of rational argument and is one of the inevitable casualties of the mental convergences of inversion. We experience no difficulty in making such discrimination when human purpose is not involved. In our sciences and in biology we separate with exaggerated care the two categories of factors, spotting when a general factor is at the basis of the spread of one species in spite of widely varying specific local conditions. But we readily accord to the latter their role as secondary cause. Anthropocentrism may be a general attitude of human self-consciousness but the European brand, misnamed humanism—which first deified Man and then in arbitrary fashion sentimentalized some of his capacities—needs to have its limits sharply redrawn.

Self-consciousness determines that mankind needs at least some sense of identity: but a second-order factor, whether of pre-history or of recorded history, fixes the individual mould. To confuse the factors can result in a grave misreading of quite recently recorded events. Any dominion over other men will impose a strain but that does not validate the latter-day self-conscious version of what is in fact a second-order factor; e.g. to-day's claim that slavery had to go because it was immoral and that therefore morality must be regarded as a general cause with the corollary that it is essential to display 'moral leadership'. By the same token the frills of liberty and authority are mistaken for their essential characteristics while other attributes of political conduct and institutions on which both liberty and authority depend, such as honesty, knowledge, and skill in administration, are dismissed as of no consequence. The so-called unintended consequences of our actions are usually the result of such misreading, not of contingency or bad luck.

It is not surprising that we misread or even overlook one of the most potent factors which have delimited the self-conscious Western mind—the European linguistic heritage which has enabled us to form rational descriptions and categories of natural and human forces and qualities. For we take our language as granted as the air we breathe or at best only become aware of both when they are beginning to be polluted. But thereby we fail to apprehend how strong are the associative links between the qualities and how strongly these are still operating upon us. This is not so with peoples such as the African negroes who have never lost the sense of immediacy that goes with mood. The impact of the Western world may have made Africans more self-consciously and assertively African but that does not mean that they will find a new satisfying identity in Western verbal concepts. As their languages illustrate, Africans' notions of order do not require the imposition of general assumptions while their need for human participation can be expressed by juxtaposition of notions as well as of bodies. The palaver demonstrates that there can be other valid mental processes of persuasion—as valid for human intercourse as European dialectics with their conceits of intellectual opposites.[2] The interminable conversations of askari bivouacs which kept me awake at night seemed at first meaningless and boring repetition. But they concluded—as far as one could establish—in a conglomerate of all viewpoints and provided that each speaker was convinced that somewhere within the conglomeration was his personal contribution, all were satisfied!

So Africa has seen its own growth of order. The elaborate social structure and methods of government of the former Dahomey kingdom exemplify how far an organism—as against an organization—can evolve from primitive instinct and juxtaposition. The absence of true verbal comparatives in an African language does not mean that its users cannot compare and discriminate: they do so by juxtaposition, while we have lost our feeling for the extent to which this can regulate human affairs, although visible evidence stares at us every day in the arrangements of fish and crustacea on quaysides and stalls from Fiji

---

[2] 'Ainsi la palabre se retrouve-t-elle à la base même de la conception africaine des relations entre les communautés. Ces dernières étant en fin d'analyse, composées d'individus, la tentation est grande de croire que la palabre n'a cours qu'entre personnes appartenant à des groupes differents. Il n'en est rien. Et le dialogue se retrouve à tous les niveaux de l'activité individuelle.

'Dès qu'une difficulté surgit entre intérêts opposés, l'Africain a recours au dialogue et aux contacts directs. Lorsque l'évolution d'un différend ne permet plus d'espérer une conclusion excluent l'usage de la force, le Chef de Famille, de Village ou de Tribu, est tenu de réunir un aréopage.'
President Ahmadou Ahidjo of the Cameroon Republic addressing Chatham House, 8.5.63.

to Fife. The great orderly movements of baboons with their scouts and advance guards hugging terrain and occupying tactical heights, the main herd moving steadily along the axis in advance, and the careful deployment of flank and rearguards show that at even earlier stages of human evolution, the patterns of symmetry must have been in existence: Camberley's formulation of military doctrine has only resulted in instinctive caution being replaced by self-conscious doubt and blue posteriors by red tabs.

To Europeans, on the other hand, proportionality has become as essential to thought as air is to life, so that although comparatives and superlatives as our most recent linguistic creations vary between even cognate tongues, we cannot express ourselves coherently without them. We assume that in the nature of things there is a possibility of exceeding or being exceeded by, and that therefore there must be a mean. Even in our comparisons 'best' implies limitation and a mean, whereas there exist human societies in whose languages there is no 'best' but only very good and very very good, and one can go on adding 'very's': there are absolutes but no proportion and no mean. The proverbial cautions of experience and instinct will serve well enough as guides and can also win assent—as they sometimes still can among Europeans when our deductive logic with its emphasis on proof and refutation fails to do so.

In traditional Africa there are few words which are purely descriptive and few verbs merit the neutral European equivalents in the dictionaries and grammar books compiled by Western teachers and scholars. The narrative and present 'tenses' turn out to be conjugations for moods of detachment and participation, so that when the same tale is told afresh to a new audience the same words take on new emphasis and colour. African verbal modes of describing experience can convey knowledge adequate for the purpose, even if Europeans who do not share this purpose find difficulty in disentangling what is the kernel of 'fact'.

When our languages are taken from their European context, their subsequent evolution and fate are the best clue to the forms of consciousness persisting among non-European peoples. The spread of English in tropical Africa will not, as the *Times Literary Supplement* seems firmly to believe, produce a black Shakespeare or Galsworthy. British expatriate teachers will be disappointed when the African renaissance they promise us on the basis of their Sixth Form's performance of *Macbeth* fails to emerge. There will no doubt be telling of tales and setting them down in books: the East African coast has been doing this since Arab days. But the combination of reasoning and insight which stimulated imagination and intellectual initiative at certain periods of Europe's history will never be repeated in African self-consciousness. The pattern of ideas which delimited European civilization will not emerge in an identical second form in any time-scale left to civilized humanity. Babel stands guard against a replication of our intellectualized self-image of Man and it can be accepted that mankind's diversity of responses to its memories will endure as long as its diverse linguistic heritage.

The curious leftover of imperialism—that somehow we can re-possess the African or anyone else by forcing his mind into our mould of language and thus obliging him to adopt our image of the world—ignores the factor of self-consciousness itself. *His* image may thereby be rudely altered but *ours* will not take its place and in the end we may regret that we interfered. Our hopes of educating non-Europeans to 'see' or to 'understand' are born of the illusion that literacy creates a different quality of knowing. The highly literate man may indeed have at his disposal an additional means of conveying his heightened consciousness of self but his style of knowing differs in degree rather than in kind from that of the less literate members of his own society. Our written language does not abstract from speech: the abstraction was in the speech and the writing only provided new symbolic possibilities.

We go even further off the rails when we talk about 'low definition imagery of the audile-tactile' mode of primitive societies.[3] The audile-tactile mode, as those who share experiences with Africans soon realize, permits in its own way a very high definition. The propagation of our 'values' through print not only fails to communicate their intuitive element but may even distort them dangerously for highly self-conscious members of another linguistic tradition. There is no harm in our pos-sessing a world picture which gratifies our inner ego and which we thereby think is life-enhancing. But we must not conclude that our version of Utopia will automatically be the prized human value of others. The disillusionment is proving cruel for all parties.

The chief actors on the African stage are as imitative as the rest of mankind and know that they are expected to have an African

[3] Marshall McLuhan, *The Gutenberg Galaxy* (Routledge & Kegan Paul, 1962), p. 39.

personality—some of them probably scratch their heads over *Encounter*. But it is at their peril that they lose their sense of immediacy. Coming out of Chatham House some years ago after listening to the apostle of negritude, President Senghor of Senegal, I ran into my ex-tutor with the same light in his eyes as he used to have after those pre-war conferences on 'The European Mind'. 'Values do come through,' he exulted and I knew that it had done his heart good to hear M. Senghor, who had been one of his students at the École Normale, talking about '*symbiose*'. But for M. Senghor, symbiosis has more than a philosophical connotation: he retains the reins of power by sensing the moods of his subjects, by anticipating conspiracy before it is formulated and crushing revolt before it can be planned. For all the time the key question for Africans is: 'What are we to each other?' The self-conscious images which they will try to present to each other in accordance with their moods will shape the African 'personality' of tomorrow but only through to-day's immediacies.

Although Africa may have been the home of the immediate ancestors of *homo sapiens*, the anthropological and archæological record shows that from the era when clearly differentiated groups of men existed on earth, Africa's techniques of tool- and weapon-making have lagged behind those of Euro-Asia for periods of tens of thousands of years. No Western excuses about lost civilizations can explain this away, nor can interludes of slavery and colonialism which were no harsher nor longer than the corresponding handicaps of caste and serfdom among other peoples of the world. For a time after *uhuru* Africans may be ready to brandish our constitutional definitions in the belief that they also contain our magic. But as the illusory surface left by colonial rule breaks up, arbitrariness erupts. The disruption of older instinctual ways and the weakening of the family, inevitable only because of the development of modern communications, have left a widespread emotional insecurity throughout the former colonial Africa and this can hardly form the basis of rationality as Europe has known it. The return to tribalism will not be a natural one but in its barbarities will possess, as in Haiti, aspects of degeneracy. There will certainly be aggression and subjugation, and since human relationships will be dominant, there will be loyalty and obedience. And since personal leadership is maintained by skilful use of power, some stability may eventually be restored to human life.

But we should be doing too much violence to our own sense of identity if we tried to stretch our own concepts of political purpose in terms which would satisfy Africa. In thus making 'intellectual concessions' we only betray our own ideas, and the Africans will regard this as surrender since they will not reconcile the 'concessions' within any conceptual framework of their own. We can share skills which are a matter of imitative teaching. But the myths and symbols of African mood can be shared by us on little more than the level of biological intuition. And significantly enough it is as a sex-symbol that the negro is continually forced on the West by both negrophiles and negrophobes—neither good for his sense of identity nor for ours.

We can agree with Africans in the terms of their palaver on the differences in things. For if instinct denies them detachment it helps them to retain their sense of the particular and of diversity. And instinct may be more important in the daily matters of 'human dignity' than generalized ideas. Our self-created doubts with their itch to tear others down breed jealousies and malice. In sensing that certainty comes not from universality but from the individual thing, the Africans are at least in harmony with Hume. Up to this point we can share their human insights.

The magic world which helped mankind through the long transition from animalism to animism and which still exists over much of Africa, is primitive only in so far as it persists among primitives. But a contemporary society equipped with modern technology can still flourish in a framework of magic custom, as Japan illustrates. For in the human mind, as the structure of even the most primitive languages reveals, there is a marked capacity to create self-sufficient entities. It existed before men uncovered magical explanations for the world, otherwise they could never have fashioned their tools. This implies that human consciousness can recognize forms so that the transmutability of things and people could give way to neutral attributes and forces. In the Western Indo-European languages the feminine gender notions for natural forces became abstractions and neuter nouns increasingly took over the description of objects. This step to a clear recognition of the separate nature of consciousness and environment has led us to the conception of an external reality to be grasped by an objective order of thought.

Not so the rest of mankind! The forbears of the present peoples of Asia never completed the decisive mental process which accepts a notion of existence independently of the subject. Objects may possess for them an aspect or essence of otherness but belong to no separate realm of objectivity. The reality of the world resides within the individual as part of his essence. Like our own, Eastern civilizations have pretensions to universality. More sophisticated versions of juxtaposition and adaptation than Africa could evolve have resulted in notions which appear to control individual behaviour and social forms. And like the West, both Chinese and Indians frequently fail to distinguish between first-order factors of human consciousness and those second-order ones which derive from their subjective notions about men and society. But with greater powers of mental endurance and a higher endowment of skills, the East can venture further than Africa in adopting our techniques without imperilling its essential core.[4] And this core, common to all its constituent peoples, from the most primitive to the most highly evolved, is a consciousness centred on the subject with its corollary of an aversion to grappling with external reality by means of ideas. And since this consciousness remains unimpaired, they too are liable to confuse cause and outcome.

No doubt if the second-order factors of Western Europe had not taken their historical forms, the East might have been on the way to establishing a world ascendancy. For although the instinctive basis of Eastern civilization may have stood in the way of scientific discovery, it did not prevent and even fostered the elaboration of techniques based on an intimate sense of the relationship of mind and body. Where a feeling for material—such as a sense of surface—is highly developed and where the subtle drawing of analogies between men and natural phenomena becomes a conscious culture in itself, both skills and arts will progress as they never could in the crude earthiness of African negro society. But if China did not extend her inventiveness into the realm of scientific experiment, it was because she lacked the cast of mind which can move between particular instance and general category. And to assimilate the process of Western theoretical objectivity, the East would have to abandon its essential core and not even its most adaptive people—the Japanese—show any sign of doing this. The East will continue to take from our material achievements and develop their application, and while we can have broad contact with its peoples at all levels, the continuing Western process of

---

[4] 'East' may appear to be a rather loose expression. In the present context it is used to describe the civilizations of India, China, and Japan and the communities of South-East Asia affected by Indian and Chinese conquest or penetration. The wide racial and cultural differences in aptitudes and skills do not alter the fundamentally subject-centred nature of the consciousness of the peoples.

the analysis of the data of human experience and their reconstruction as fresh concepts is not one which the East could or would want to share. The pioneer minds will remain Western.

Criticisms of European policies and actions couched by Eastern political leaders in ethical terms borrowed from us—such as the late unlamented Nehru was wont to do—can be read by us in the light of their own expediencies. Further we need not accompany them, but instead consider what is expedient for us. If the Chinese and Russians foundered over authoritative interpretations of Marxism, could we really have expected, or still expect, the Chinese to have assimilated at various stages of their history the implications of second-order European notions as restated by Marx, Lenin, and their successors?

This had earlier been the fate of the ethical notions interwoven with Christian imagery in the Western consciousness. A mystery Middle East cult of dying and resurrecting gods, the historical descendant of sacrificial rites based on fear, could never have established an ascendancy over the minds of those whose evolution from primitive animism to secularism had followed a different course. Nestorian missionaries, Jesuits with their clockworks and astrolabes, American Baptists with their pills and bandages, although appreciated for their human qualities, could never make the Christian concept of redemption convincing to the Chinese. It could not be otherwise with Marxism. It is only surprising that Western governments, particularly the British Foreign Office with its troupe of old China hands, refused in 1959 to accept the firm intelligence of the growing Sino-Soviet dispute and recognition had to wait another three years until it suited the Chinese to announce it themselves.

The Chinese may accept the notions of conversion and of coming to terms. But throughout their history they have never even attempted to grapple with the Western idea that foreign policy consists of choices. This would clash with their notion of the inner unity of the subject. At most they will accept tactical moves which can be presented or explained as cunning, but never that there can be a rational alternative course towards a world Communist order as the result of some new 'objective' intrusive factor such as the possession of nuclear weapons or African and Asian developments. 'Objective factors of history', the essence of Western Marxist jargon, are excluded from the Eastern form of consciousness: once within the Marxist process the Chinese must follow the whole process and nothing but the process; their 'how logic' is concerned with rules of conduct as against the Western 'what logic' which forms the basis of our rational discussion.[5] Brezhnev can create syllogisms from subject-predicate relationships based on the verb 'to be'. Where there is no 'to be' but only the word *shih*, which by its presence or absence adds or takes away emphasis, revisionism is not to be justified by logical argument.

Chinese utterance, like our own, still shows traces of its origins in the magical and mythical cast of thought but by continually extending its power to suggest conduct, to convince, and to convert, it also stands up to our test of time as a language of civilization. The human feelings for duration and for the physical dimensions of environmens are not linked to an abstract conception of time as a steady progrest of similar moments nor to a notion of space as an abstraction of linked elements. But they are satisfied by definitions of activity conditioned by the here and now, for which there are always corresponding symbols. Attachment to natural environment means that the individual remains strongly attached to objects by an immediate relationship such as imitation, so that he still feels invested with their qualities or invests them with his own. This sustains the skills of Mongol peoples and bears witness to a form of consciousness as abiding as that of the West.

And this guarantees to the Chinese the possibility of survival both as a society and as individuals, whereas the subject-centred consciousness of the peoples of India brings them again and again to the verge of social disintegration and self-destruction from which they have usually been saved by outside intervention or conquest. The skill, cunning, and self-seeking of the individual—whether Hindu, Sikh, Patel, or member of some other of India's myriad cults—stand out in sharp contrast to the high-flown sentiments of his professed faith. Daily realities follow one path while the disciplines of introspective detachment allow for the luxury of subjective withdrawal from troublesome obligations. Disconcerting, no doubt, for those who assume that the spoken word corresponds to inward motive. But the Indian way is intended neither for intruders nor for export: it is the product of a form of inversion which concerns only Indians themselves. The exploration of truth by action which characterized the great Aryan movements of the second millenium B.C. ended in India with their

[5] The expressions are from Prof. Alf Sommerfelt's discussion of Chang Tang Sun's studies of the relations between Chinese language and Chinese logic and where they differ from European categories. *Diachronic and Synchronic Aspects of Language* (Mouton & Co., 1962), pp. 130–2.

military conquests and the later search for truth through reasoning never began.

On the centenary of Mahatma Gandhi's birth in October 1969, there were laments that his dream of a proud and tolerant India had ended in a nightmare of religious slaughter and sordid scrambles for power among the Congress politicians who had been his personal disciples. This is no new phenomenon in India's history. The Buddhist religion, which might have taught the Indians worldly compassion, significantly enough disappeared in its land of origin. As an export to China, Japan, and South-East Asia, Buddhism degenerated into such over-simplified forms that it can be recognized only by the idols and was long ago absorbed by local superstitions and subordinated to the needs of local rulers. The arts, which flourish among the extrovert Chinese who love to express and communicate through their creations, remain crude physical affairs in India.

As the Westernized superstructure of India finally collapses and the need for a strong temporal authority is increasingly sensed, the confused political consciousness of younger Indians, their admiration for social hierarchy, and their personal material ambition will make them tractable material for authoritarianism. The parents dabbled in their time with European liberalism and socialism. For the sons, Hindu atavism is likely to be the main consolation while they serve whatever new rulers history may bring them. The hardships of daily life will be horrifying but acceptable. What De Toqueville noted, still applies: 'Famine kills one third of the population of Bengal, three to four million men. They die like heroes amid the herds which their religion forbids them to touch: the same men who flee by the thousand before one European! What one calls their weakness is therefore not fear of death, but rather absence of reason for braving it.'[6]

Yet India is not an 'underdeveloped' country. To say so is arrogance on our part. According to her own terms, her mind is still active and the process is not terminated. Nor should the Eastern feeling for the filigree of personal duties, which shows itself in the giving and taking of gifts, be considered as inferior to the Western concept of contract with its rationalization of right by observance and of wrong by breach. In the context of instinct-orientated societies adjusting to ever-changing necessities, it may prove a surer guide in preserving

[6] *Notes On A Visit To India.*

K

human relationships. Where nature is accepted as permeating all existence, there is no room for freedom of the will: there can only be the opposite of what is determined by instinct. Freedom for the East thus means freedom of consciousness, whereas in Europe it means freedom of decision and action. An unburdened mind gives the East-erner a sense of being free while Western strivings for freedom tend to finish up in the straitjacket of conceptualized historical definitions of civic liberty. A prearranged sequence is assumed by us: it is not an Asian assumption.

Where the Western aim is to create unity or at least discover unifying principles which would explain apparent multiplicity, the Asian accepts isolated or juxtaposed data. To our universality he still opposes his particular. This latter approach has an appearance of modesty and tolerance, although at times it can be rudely disturbed by violent short circuits if the particular identity is threatened. But it is also characterized by dignity and reserve in the face of necessity. We should not despise this attitude, for the concept of freedom of the will which we oppose to nature's causality can still not be rationally demonstrated. It is only contingency which can escape necessity so that in the end, like Thomas Carlyle's American lady friend, we find we have to accept the universe.

But precisely because this dilemma does not exist for Asians, there is utter incompatibility between our respective civilizations. They are subjectively at rest while with our concern for objects we are objectively not free. As the ideas to which we have shackled ourselves break up, we too shall be dispersed while Asians can remain themselves. Even after three generations of British-type schooling, the Asians from East Africa remain the closest knit and most exclusive Hindu, Sikh, Patel and Ismaili communities anywhere in the world. And now in the name of our ideas they move into Britain in sufficient numbers to maintain their particular loyalties and duties while our loyalty disintegrates in the service of an alleged universality. The greatness of Western civilization came from an attempt to abolish the Self: now the others move in supported by the Self.

And dispersal of identity and disintegration of loyalty are not empty phrases without social consequences: the reaction of any society which senses that it is on such a path will be equally consequential. While the evolution of consciousness round subject in the East and outwards towards object in the West has produced apparently stable forms, it has also left whole peoples at uncertain crossroads of identity.

At some early stage in their history, the Arabs turned in on themselves so that their emotionally charged language has piled up ever higher barriers between external reality and consciousness of self, with the result that the only world that matters is a subjective one where violent outburst is the easiest escape from shallow brooding. Their military conquests brought no lasting flowering of new creations and institutions and to-day the cause of Arab unity is ever and again lost in the fierce divisiveness of self-assertion. Western technology beckons to them but is suddenly rejected with the petulant cry that it still cannot help Arabs to win their wars.

The language faithfully reflects the state of mind. Tense is hardly detached. The radicals of the verbs evoke temporary or lasting states, the 'perfect' may denote finished actions but the 'imperfect' serves as present or future and the stem itself is transmuted by minor vocalization into indicative, subjunctive, and jussive moods shading through more intensified forms into the imperative. And so the verb throws its mood through the whole sentence and the active voice—the known—can with slight change become the passive—the unknown. In his traditional society the interaction of consciousness and language served the Arab well enough. But there has been no question of mind moving from specific impressions to general, no repeated breaking and reconstruction by temporal synthesis which would create a sense of escape into wider fields of ideas. The emotional continuum which Arabic helps to sustain may satisfy the deep human need for participation but it can also suffocate the mind.[7]

The tragedy is that Arabs and Europeans come so close to each other. We are linked by some far-away Caucasoid descent, our minds as well as our territories skirt each other sufficiently closely for a love-hate relationship to develop. An educated Arab minority

---

[7] Sir Hamilton Gibb suggests that the Arabs once possessed a rational capacity. '. . . the Arab world lost the faculty of reasoning in scientific and concrete terms based upon verified postulates, and at the same time the sensitivity of its intuitive perception became blunted and its imaginative and spiritual life revolved at random.' *Studies On the Civilization of Islam* (Routledge & Kegan Paul, 1963).

He blames the Prophet for preaching a monotheism which was intellectually satisfying while emotionally stultifying. Since at the time of the emergence of Islam the Arabic language was certainly not less emotionally charged than it is to-day, it is as hard to believe in a pre-Islamic Arab rationality as in Atlantis.

from the *domaine française* of the Levant, Egypt, and the Mahgreb have acquired the superficies of European life and language and produce epigonic novels, poems, and plays. But they cannot act as a regenerative element in Arab culture since the relationship between intuition and concept which underlies our cultural creativity is absent. Modern Arabic literature remains a stilted artificial affair, perhaps because the Arabs themselves provide each other with all the drama and fiction a man could possibly absorb. The Arab intellectuals of the Europeanized fringe come no further than sensing how far we fail to live up to our own ideas but can find no reconciliation between these latter and the surging emotionalism of the Semitic mind.

So it is not surprising that the Arabs show signs of abandoning the hundred-year-old attempt to model themselves on European lines, and that they reject traditions and beliefs too different from those to which they remain intuitively linked. Islam combines with language to remain the sheet anchor of identity: without it Arabs would have neither identity nor society. The young officers who overthrow traditional rulers claiming divine sanction or descent from the Prophet, and then set out to 'modernize' their states, are before long invoking Islam as the justification of their policies: the sharia law is proclaimed as supreme over the European civil codes and contracts which might prove a barrier to their plans. Since this rejection is essentially an inversion of hate, there can never be a promise of lasting order. Lest we think the fault is on our side, let us note that the Arabs cannot even find emotional reconciliation with the Kurds now so mixed with their own stock as to be outwardly indistinguishable and sharing the same faith and the same historical conquests.

It is not only Middle Eastern communities which in historical time have in some way lost their hold on external reality without finding a satisfying subjectivity. The peoples of Latin America have for a century and a half experienced the corruption of the beliefs, ideas, institutions and organizations they inherited from the Old World and have been unable to establish a new framework of society within which they could find a reassurance of identity. Of the Spaniards themselves, with their mixture of Iberian, Phœnician, Arab, Goth and Vandal, it has been said: 'They have expanded and contracted the objective zone of their life in a dramatic rhythm: they are not inclined to industrial activity nor will they agree to live without industry. At certain moments the outward sallies, the efforts to break out of themselves . . . give rise to problems that have no normal mode of solution.'[8] But in Spain some common bond of Spanishness brings them together again in spite of individual outburst. In the overseas lands of Spanish rule, no fusion of identity has emerged. Ortega y Gasset could only see the immigrants to Argentina as 'men lacking all interior discipline, men uprooted from their native European societies where they had lived without realizing it, morally disciplined by a sort of stabilized and integral collective life'. One clear conclusion of a hundred years of Latin American political independence is that violence is not an effective instrument of social and economic change. The mystery is that any European 'intellectual' should now believe that it can still be.

There is no single Latin American state where political stability can be assumed. In Bolivia and Venezuela, politics are conducted by massacre. The Portuguese tradition offers no better prospect for although the various ethnic communities of Brazil have modified their own customs, acquired a second tongue, and enjoy tolerable separate existences, central government remains the preserve of gangsterdom or of futile rhetoricians. 'Right', 'Left', 'Progress', and 'Renovation' are phrases devoid of all content. The great wealth and ability of the peoples are directed to no constructive end. The rivalries of leadership are more important than the implementation or consolidation of policies. For over a hundred years the prevailing intellectual fashion has been a nostalgic anarchism dressed up in the latest café jargon. Latin Americans are certainly identifiable but hardly as paragons of Universal Man.

Their problem is relatively uncomplicated in comparison with that of over-heightened Jewish self-consciousness which floats like some ectoplasm in uncertain time and space. 'Jewry is not a race or religion but an obsession—an anxiety neurosis', writes Mr. Gerald Abrahams. 'The oppressed Jew however is not the saddest type. More pitiable specimens exist in emancipation. They do not know what they are, Jewish or British, Jewish or American: nor what their purpose should be.'[9] Their past tragedies may excuse their over-sensitivity and they may feel that the great European historical movements, the Reformation, the rise of the nation-state, the democratic revolutions, and finally Communism and Fascism, have not altered basic Gentile

[8] America Castro, *The Structure of Spanish Society* (Princeton University Press), p. 664.
[9] *The Jewish Mind* (Constable, 1961), pp. 327, 329.

attitudes towards them. They have of course profited from the European *trésor commun*, the growing softening of custom and behaviour
which have changed the manner if not the matter of their special
problem. But Jewish particularizing still cuts across Western universalizing, and the endeavour to maintain an identity based on the myths
of a vanished world and the relics of tribal taboos ever and again
confronts the *diaspora* with a mental contradiction for which it tries
to compensate by pointing out the anomalies of its host communities.

This is never difficult. We are all bundles of contradictions. But
the critical Jewish habit contains an inherent double-edged risk
since it is sensed by the Gentile at moments of insecurity as being a
deliberate attempt to cast doubts on his identity. Since the greatest
threat to European Jewry, namely Naziism, was itself destroyed by
those whose strongest weapon was a wholesome instinct for their own
heritage, the Jewish intellectual finds himself in an untenable position
by claiming historical privilege while denouncing historicism in
others, appealing to general ethical notions which he believes would
serve the purposes of his own community, but attacking notions which
he finds less attractive as 'holism' or 'Hegelianism'. The quick instinct
which his very survival required in a potentially hostile environment
tends to lead to major misjudgements in more relaxed settings. For
a self-conscious Jew can himself never relax.

Since the misnamed anti-Semitism preceded not only Naziism
but even Christianity, feudalism, Renaissance, democracy and nationalism, its cause is not to be found in religions, ideas and theories,
nor will its rebuttal be found in them either. So there need be no
Western Gentile inhibition to the frank discussion of the problems
which arise from the Jews' own confusions and contradictions. Until
the Palestine issue introduced a power-political factor into the Middle
East, the Jews in Arab lands were treated as but slightly deviant
cousins: in Iranian cities they were another corporation of merchants
suffering from the occasional cupidity of the rulers as did Armenians
and others. The problem of identity arises only in the Western world.
For while a Jew's sensitivity to the personal reactions and needs of
those who might be either protector, oppressor, patron, customer,
friend or foe became as highly developed as his self-consciousness,
there is a curious Jewish obtuseness to those subtle psychological
shifts which herald the sloughing off of one set of ideas and the emergence of an embryonic new order. Or perhaps it is not curious! The
dialogue of opposites is the antithesis of the Jewish intuitive approach.

But it nevertheless leaves him at the crossroads when a new setting of society throws up new allegiances. At this point the scorner's chair becomes a hot seat.

The Jewish belief that they have been in the vanguard of human thought thus turns out to be another myth. While the Old Testament may have provided Europe with symbols round which the first theologies and intellectual systems of the West were built and to which European artists could apply their imagination, the European Jews buried themselves deeper in obscure exegesis. If this assisted in the immediate preservation of their own communal loyalty, it also meant that their leaders sensed too late the significance of the transition from the semi-tribal groupings of the late Roman Empire to the first feudal loyalties, of the rise of ordered rule by charter and legal definition and finally the new emphasis in state and society of the new national consciousness. For Western thought preserves itself through change. The negative aspects of nineteenth-century liberal emancipation could not provide the European Jews with the security they sought and its positive aspects were lost to them by the bigotry of community leaders who preferred to emulate the Rechabites. To-day the Jewish intellectual fashion is mainly the Lib/Lab internationalism of the thirties. Where the members of their community have secured the editorial monopoly of some publishing forum, up goes the dreary chant about Freud, Einstein, and Kafka: but the probability is that Gentile political inclinations and intellectual preferences have been loaded on to a new caravan which is already departing. This is the European Jewish tragedy and the price of rabbinical arrogance and intellectual dishonesty is paid by the decent quiet-living craftsmen and traders as they face new exile or even destruction.

For only as a European with the special status resulting from his brand of *apartheid* does the Jew possess an identity. It is understandable enough that Israel offers him an uncertain prospect. Outside Europe no Jewish community has ever made a distinctive contribution to general human achievement: the secret lies in the West. The way back to Jerusalem and Baghdad was always open even during the battles and uncertainties of the Dark Ages and of the Arab conquests. The Jewish role as an interpreter of moods, with all its agonies and triumphs, has no place in Israel: he becomes a number on a passport or an army identity card and has to work as one of many. Even the founders of Israel do not find this task easy. Archæologists to a man, they dig ever deeper in the hope of finding a past which can never be theirs. And at the same time as they struggle to rebuild Zion, the self-conscious mood of our time has intensified the myth-making of Israel's neighbours.

The Western *diaspora* will not even enjoy for long the solace of watching Israel create a vicarious identity for them. 'In half a century Israel will demographically conform to the indigenous population of the Middle East . . . in due time the Oriental wing of the World Jewry will be represented almost entirely by the Israeli society and the dialogue between Israel and the *diaspora* will distinctly echo the dialogue between East and West . . . The other important myth exploded by the realities of Israel is the myth of a unitary Jewish culture . . . Hebrew society based on the myths of the return of the tribes identified on religious bases cannot by its nature be a Western society as understood and practised by the West.'[10] The natural reaction of the *sabra* to all this is a desire to be part of a normal nation with all the limitations of normal nations, and he rejects both the notion of the uniqueness of Jewry and that of any special mission. Such phrases as 'Israel's unique claim to the support of human conscience' are for the *sabra* empty flummery.[11]

So the military victories can only be a holding operation and the needs of Israeli statecraft are more likely to add to the anxieties of the *diaspora* than diminish them. 'Multiple loyalties are desirable and it is a part of the life of free democracies to hold to the sacred difference', wrote the late Professor Norman Bentwich.[12] But while *within* the nation-state as it has evolved in Europe and in the lands of European settlement, a multiplicity of loyalties of family, group, employer, church and state are of the essence, the demands of second *external* loyalty to an entity following the expediencies of power will impose fresh strains. The Israeli *realpolitik* in Africa to counter Nasser created embarrassment among the South African Jews who had been the supporters and financiers of the Liberation war of 1948: French Jewish indignation rang hollow when President De Gaulle likewise followed what he conceived to be the French interest and switched his arms sales from Israel to the Arabs. America's power needs in the Middle East require a balancing role, not the taking of sides. The conflicts of interest throughout the world will unfortunately not free

[10] Ferdynand Zweig, *Israel: The Sword And The Harp* (Heinemann, 1969), pp. 37, 195, 198.
[11] Phrase in a letter by a Mr. George Steiner in *The Times*, 25.8.69.
[12] *The Jews In Our Time* (Pelican).

the Jews as a community from suspicion of where their loyalty lies. Dr. Nahum Goldmann, President of the World Jewish Congress, does his co-religionists no service by admitting that he has possessed seven passports. A purely mythical identity only creates irrationality. Assimilation into the increasingly secular Gentile society of our time is still the only rational solution; the Jews owe it to the Gentiles as well as to themselves.

The Jewish dilemma of loyalty is of two-fold interest since its facets catch and illuminate correspondences in the whole European process. We too need a backward look—mythical or not—to reassure ourselves that in the midst of change and renewal we are the same persons. For unlike the sterility of Judaism, it is primarily through the illusion of freedom of decision and the consciousness of change that European identity renews itself. Sometimes the turn of events has swept a whole community into a new grouping while their communal consciousness was but half-developed. The Burgundians, as far as one can establish, feel no resentment at the loss of their embryonic nation-state and their assimilation into the greater community of France: the shifting allegiance of their dukes appears to have had its counterpart in the comfortable acceptance by their subjects of whatever had been decided for them. Swiss society on the other hand bears the hallmark of the late mediæval world—male exclusivity, tight-knit family hierarchies, the burghers' pride in hard-won material status— and Swiss democracy seems the natural descendant of the revolt against the Hapsburgs, the last and most successful of the oath-taking confederations of the Middle Ages: through the process of institutional change the Swiss retain their identity.

So the balance of permanence and change is never certain; it is the secondary factors which maintain historical identities and institutions while their weakening throws the peoples involved back on to the basic primary needs for participation and authority. The magnitude of the changes demanded of or inflicted on German society over the past hundred years resulted in a tragedy of *Sturm und Drang*, as a restless and dynamic people—endowed with a language combining emotional invocation, wide-sweeping generalization, and action-charged utterance—struggled with the consequences of political unification, territorial disruption, revolution, reaction, victory, defeat, extreme permissiveness and inevitable counter-action. If Germans now show a marked aversion to Left-Wing radicalism, they sense only too well that it contains the peril of chaos renewed.

And Western Europe confronts to the East an identity which seems both unchanging and ambiguous. In spite of fashions in political vocabulary and surface ethnic and linguistic variations and discrepancies, the Russian sense of 'Russianness' has never been more marked. In the case of a people still speaking their language of prehistory, there is no emotional gulf between intuitive utterance and intellectual abstraction. Russian internal affairs are not to be explained solely in terms of ideology nor of power and hierarchy: we continually come up against the riddle of what in Russian consciousness is regarded as a valid objective concept and at what point intuition has taken over or let go. Even when one presents one's papers in perfect order to a Russian sentry, the uneasy feeling remains that he will sense or see something of which the traveller is not aware: and over the open broadboned Slav countenance, suspicion will suddenly throw a dark cloud.

The gap between the 'West' and Soviet Russia at times seems wide in theory and sometimes appears to close. Points of view seem near but agreement proves impossible. Western military strategy and diplomacy try to work on the assumption that the rulers of Russia share apprehensions akin to our own. But though the Russians may fear war, if it comes the opportunities it offers for conquest and booty are uppermost. The first glimpses that Western Europe had of the Russian army in 1945 were of marching infantry columns with their horse transport piled with loot, the commanding officers in their two-horsed carts with their women folk and domestic paraphernalia, the soldiers with cardboard suitcases of junk bargaining in the market squares of the occupied towns. They were as good Marxists as Englishmen are good Christians—which leaves plenty of room for manœuvre. Their sense of being Russian and their intuitive roots of culture remain intact.

Our long-term assessments of Russia's likely future are clouded by our determination to prevent the political dogma of liberalism being submitted to the tests of fallibility. Liberal ideas, we believe, are capable of infinite adaptation, are progressive, and do not lose their validity as the result of new inventions. Not so Marxism, we maintain: its ideas will be demonstrated as invalid in a society of technologists, scientists, and managers. If a number of our own leading scientists claim to be Marxists and do not thereby seem to lose their scientific acumen, this is dismissed as a personal aberration, a luxury we can afford within the framework of liberal ideas. And if it is pointed out again that acceptance of Darwinism, modern genetics and physics can be combined with the belief that men are created in the image of some god and that magic notions such as 'evil' can be introduced into rational argument, this is excused as a 'traditional attitude'.

Russians can cope with the same discrepancies. Their identity has not become the prisoner of ideas nor has the subject become engulfed by objects. We should therefore be wary of anticipating ideological revolt or counting on a younger Russian generation rejecting the imposed ideas of Marxism. Such revolt may seem appropriate to a human consciousness which finds its ultimate realization in objective concepts. But the emotional factor of the interplay of a child's experience and its intuitive relationship with words will never be the same for Russian and Briton: the need to assert itself against parental restraints and notions will find different modes of expression. The present cult among younger Russian poets and writers of taking up a *Gewissensjude* seems to be related more to their ambivalent revelling in guilty association than to some fresh spread of tenderness.

But there will be change inside Russia because new objects will enter Russian consciousness and concept and intuition will battle for their possession. Stalinism in its original form can never return although there will be other forms of arbitrary rule which Russians will have to endure in the future as they have done in the past. And over its own peoples and those it has conquered or 'liberated' will loom the moral and intellectual vacuum of Russian rule. 'The Russian autocracy has neither a European nor an Oriental parentage' wrote Joseph Conrad, '—a true desert harbouring no spirit either of the East or of the West.' It is this sense of void which has motivated the highest level of Russian 'defectors' to the West over the last decade. Beneath the rulers is an ever-pliant layer of petty tyrants and sycophantic stewards. To-day the rule of the stewards will not be seriously challenged from within. Even if they fall out among themselves as has happened several times since the Bolshevik Revolution, the possibility of new revolutions can only arise if they fail in the face of an external challenge.

Since the rulers of Russia share the same insight as those they rule, they are well aware of the emotional power which can be released against them. They will regard the Yevtuschenkos and Solzhenitsyns with as much suspicion as the Czarist ministers treated nineteenth-century writers, although still allowing them a limited freedom. The state censors passed Schiller's *Die Räuber* for stage performance but refused their stamp to the same sentiments in the dramas of contemporary writers: but all—censors, authors, actors, and audiences—revelled in the guilty enjoyment of conspiracy, and the rulers still worried. The cult of personality is easily countered in the case of outward aggrandizement: the inflation or deflation of the inner man requires other alembics. The Kremlin diatribes against the intelligentsia represent anxieties which cannot be reduced to card-indexed items in the secret police records.

However, this does not necessarily presage a general questioning of values—a 'spiritual crisis' in Western style. The crisis of Russian inner needs is more likely to express itself as personal reaction against arbitrariness in human relations than as a call for institutional change. None of the present literary rebels will push their rebellion any further than did Ehrenbourg: for there is always the solace of introspective regret attainable through a language which transmutes easily from tense to aspect and then to mood. And with minds where the transitions between tense and mood have never been broken, even Marxism can be tolerable, for it is not a set of values but a method of reasonings. Its goals are for the future; it is a plausible soap box or academic verbal tool for putting forward cause and effect relationships, and by the test of the here and now it appears less vulnerable than Western European philosophies of value.

So if there is effective challenge to the rule of the stewards it will be an external one. So far their tanks have taken care of Hungarians, Czechs, Poles, and East Germans. But now they have exposed themselves to a degree which is unique in Russian history even to a point where they have made Arabs, Africans, Indians and Chinese arbiters of their power games. The Kremlin may regard assertive self-conscious human diversity as a force to be exploited tactically to undermine Western European and American power and influence. Russian warships may now patrol the seven seas, their reconnaissance-strike planes establish themselves in new Asian and African bases, and their military techniques find testing grounds near the strategic narrows of the world. But they may have given hostages to fortune. In the Middle East, Russian policy becomes dependent on the uncertain Arab mood, in Africa on primitive symbiosis, and on the inconsistencies and corruption of Indian politicians and officials. Mobutu threw the Russians out of the Congo, Nasser's death meant an agonizing reappraisal, the money, goods and weapons poured out on the feckless Soekarno were all wasted, Cambodian 'neutrality' swung from Communist to American camp. Using all their skill as traders and entrepreneurs, the Chinese find means of countering Kremlin moves.

So if the Western notion of Universal and Equal Man has to yield to the recognition of other forms of human consciousness, the future for his Marxist cousin is no rosier. The many deviant groups, particularly in the Western world, who continue to label themselves Marxists, correspond to no category that Marx, Lenin, Trotsky, or even Mao would ever accept as such: in their own way they herald the atomization of Communism. So in a world perspective the power confrontations of what was once the Cold War may have a positive outcome if it means the end of the two versions of Man which have brought about so much betrayal.

But we cannot remain passive. The dissident groups can still be disruptive and even destructive in societies where human loyalties have weakened. The servants of the Kremlin in France and Italy are powerful enough to tear apart the alliances of the Western world at a time of crisis. Yet it is in conflict that men find each other's true worth and these dangers offer their own opportunities. The break-up of the universal notions of imperial Rome opened the way to new allegiances. In Asia and Africa the resurgent identities of men's past are showing up the fiction of a wider loyalty to 'Man'. What can the Western world posit as the step towards recovering its own sense of identity and at the end of the road glimpse the legitimacy which will hold loyalties?

VII. Delimiting the Future

VII. Delimiting the Future

These identities bequeathed from a past which—in spite of J. H. Plumb—shows no signs of dying, point to a plurality of human loyalties none of them likely to accommodate the myths of 1776. On the contrary, it is the New World which is most beset by ideological hobgoblins. Since what happens in the United States will react powerfully on Western European allegiances, we must needs be sympathetic watchers as the Americans attempt to exorcize or placate the spirits which are disturbing their dream. Although more given than Europeans to asking themselves what they are, they should not on that account be regarded as inwardly insecure. No member of the human race has in fact so well marked an identity tab as an American and only English jealousy could make Dr. Samuel Johnson say: 'I could love all humanity, Sir, save only an American.' The American success over two hundred years in founding a state, settling a Continent, facing up to the issues of slavery and civil war, digesting millions of heterogeneous elements, developing their own unmistakable attributes, and emerging as the world's greatest material power, is remarkable by any human standard.

Even at the time of the War of Independence the letters and diaries of North American settlers and soldiers—whether of British, Dutch, or German descent—strike a different sturdy tone from those of the British and Hessian officers and men they were fighting. It is a comfort to know that 'Americanism' antedates 1776 and that the characteristic traits we now associate with the American people have a human and not an ideological origin: this holds out the hope that they can survive even if their ideas perish. Yet while Americans reach out into space, there is a growing sense among them that the old identity is disappearing and there is no certain sign of the new. The simplest test of loyalty and patriotism—the schoolchild's salute to his country's flag—is rejected by increasing numbers. The myths of the past, of pioneering days, of independence, of civil war, and of conquest, are losing their power because Americans have lost confidence in the present.

L

Ontologically speaking, the whole American adventure aimed at an objectivity of action and one would thus expect American self-consciousness to have produced a formulation of activism which would be unshakeably self-confident. The system of government was admirably designed to achieve this even though the motives of the founders had been to restrain rather than encourage acts of State. In practice the separation of powers gave the Executive a clear field for action through which the practical politician could advance to office via pork-barrel distributions to imaginative and decisive heights. But now a whole pseudo-objective vocabulary drawn from social sciences, communications, and technology has filtered into American political usage, displacing human analogies, and being passed off as an accurate description for human motivation and decision. The language of power assessment degenerates into what those not yet caught up in the process call 'Cherokee'.

For a time the totality of the American strategic commitment furthered the illusion that 'Cherokee' could be a substitute for the objective analysis of global policy factors. The two sharpest quarrels in which the United States has been involved over the last fifteen years—with China and Cuba—happened to fit in with this picture. They also happened to be emotional issues where the United States saw itself as the rejected lover. Diabolism seemed the only explanation and since the concurrent power confrontation with Soviet Russia also appeared to fit this, American policy-making, for all the pseudo-objectivity of state papers and strategic assessments, evaded facing the fact that at no time could Chinese, Cuban, or Soviet reality correspond to American notions of 'Man'. The odd working diplomat, such as Mr. George Kennan, who was prepared to admit some virtues in one's opponents and some shortcomings in oneself, was left out in the cold.

But now the United States has reached a stage in its history where it has to admit that it is in no position to offer any lasting alternative to any group of mankind anywhere. There is no rival form of idealized humanity to be defeated either in the field or in debate. The world may not want colonialism or Communism but neither does it want progress as conceived by Americans. Superiority of physical destructive power can no longer be deployed to support ideological, juridical, or political absolutes but at best can be effective in situations of balance where American self-interest is clearly defined, and even this can hardly be done without domestic acrimony. Moral attitudes which get out of step with power and diplomatic moves become doubly damaging. This requires a tricky appraisal from a people geared to action and whose favourite slogan is 'Let's go!'

The tools for appraisal are to hand and there is more than a suspicion among Americans themselves that the ideas associated with the image of Man have become dehumanized. For the United States does not face to the same extent as does Britain the problem of a number of little political, social, and academic establishments each tucked away in its own little self-satisfied enclave. Nor is there a superstition that ignorance is in the public interest; the right to know is acknowledged and it is official policy to make archives on recent history available to the student of contemporary affairs. There is active interchange between business career and political office-holding and between government and university at all ages and levels. There should theoretically be less of the self-centredness and deliberate exclusion of fresh minds and factual knowledge which too often characterize European governments.

And so far the direst prophecies of what could happen in the United States have never been fulfilled because Americans have lived in communities where intuitive human relationships have countered extremist ideas or halted arbitrariness and outrage. But now this brake is being dismantled as community bonds are ruptured and are replaced by artificial contrivance. The individual can either conform to the artificial stimulants or, sensing their contrivance, turn inwards in an unhappy inversion. Older generations had still Mr. Dooley's horse-sense scepticism to counter some of the fantasies about Man. But since the images now evoked in the language of public debate have become as synthetic as the flavour of American pies, the current of anarchism which has been a noticeable undertow in American life for almost a hundred years comes more strongly to the surface: the sense that the human race is turning into a mass of atomized individuals results in a cry for the abolition of Man, to use Norman Ginsberg's phrase. This strain of anarchism at times becomes obsessive and its practitioners rather smelly, but it does carry the Romantic process to its logical conclusion with the American version of Young Werther claiming total alienation. The question is whether the American Werther can make a fresh beginning before general exasperation starts an indiscriminate blowing out of brains.

Loyalty to leadership has suffered in the meantime from the attempts of United States governments to present images of themselves which fit in with the requirements of phoneyness. Since these progres-

sively cease to carry conviction they have aroused disgust and hate
verging almost on the paranoic. The Kennedy administration could
never make up its mind on this score: in the end it plumped for the
phoney.[1] Chiasmus and other conceits of antithesis were worked over
and over again—the tension of opposites, they called them. White
House assemblies, where Beethoven and negro jazz were presented
in succession to an audience of over-dressed New York impresarios
and public-relations men, were described by lick-spittle journalists as a
'New Versailles', a leading daily which refused to support the image
was ostentatiously excluded from Presidential reading matter, and it
became hard to say whether the President's wife was more concerned
with her image or doctored versions of what it should have been.
And in the end a paranoic's bullet did find its mark in the image.

Yet there had been a growing unease at this all-out venture in
phoneyness even among those who conceded Kennedy's merits as
a man. Perhaps the virtue of Johnson's term of office with its more
natural flavour of pork-barrel days was that it offered a respite from
Madison Avenue manipulations. It enabled Americans to adjust to
the sort of reality which is now presenting a not-too-pleasant face.
Outlets have still to be found for action which indulgence has failed
to provide. A society in which the crime rate is rising at four times
that of population growth without any apparent relation to poverty
or racial minority problems has to find such outlets.

But other activists have also moved in. For all the time there had
never been a Man, there had been little homogeneity among the
men. The cities in which the negroes have been steadily congregating
for almost thirty years have become the haunts of the disinherited
and the alienated, while the prosperous whites move out to suburban
myths of gracious living bolstered up by a proliferation of gadgets.
In a society where dignity is at a discount there will be little sense of

---

[1] The subtle process by which a man is subordinated to the needs of office is
illustrated by recalling what Kennedy (or his speech writer) had to say on
illusion and myth in his speech at Yale University in June, 1962:

'The great enemy of the truth is very often not the lie—deliberate,
contrived and dishonest—but the myth—persistent, persuasive and un-
realistic. Too often we hold fast to the clichés of our forebears. We subject
all facts to a prefabricated set of interpretation. We enjoy the comfort of
opinion without the discomfort of thought.

'Mythology distracts us everywhere—in government as in business, in
politics as in economics, in foreign affairs as in domestic policy.'

achieving 'human dignity' even under the most favourable material conditions. 'An American Virgin would never dare command: an American Venus would never dare exist.'[2] So now that the negro is fully self-conscious and resentful of his inferior status, what prospect is there for him? The 1963 prediction of the United States Attorney-General, then Mr. R. F. Kennedy, that racial disturbances would go on for ten years and which shocked so many Americans, now seems an under-statement: no end is in sight.

This however points to disintegration and degradation rather than revolution. Sustained militancy requires an effort of leadership and organization which—even if supported by white Americans who have developed hates against their own kind—would be a new departure for the negro. Relapse into indulgence has not been merely an inevitable escape for the American coloured communities: it has been one of the main characteristics of African society. That until negroes are given responsibility they cannot develop a sense for it remains for the moment an excuse for the apparent deficiency of the theory of human equality rather than a piece of evidence. The negro 'intellectual', once he has been given a status, rapidly tucks himself into whatever niche white society offers him, the negro political representatives hardly live up to their responsibilities although in fairness they may claim that they have only modelled themselves on their white colleagues, and the more popular crusader becomes an *exalté* at the very moment he should be showing restraint and calculation and is consequently bumped off.

A few negro show pieces are carefully propped up and maintained in Federal posts to be produced in dinner jackets at State Department receptions. They are decent souls and meet the needs of Scandinavians who ask the United States to send a black envoy to prove some moral point or another: but old complexes make them uncertain subjects for experiments in responsibility. Even when light-skinned men are transferred from the clerical side of diplomacy and faced with the type of African situation which a European or African district officer takes in his stride by applying either symbiosis or the whip, the result is saddening. Indeed when negro blood has become sufficiently diluted, those in whose veins it flows slip with relief into the nondescript ranks of the olive-tanned city proletariat. Or at some point negro militancy may produce a nation-wide reaction among a people

[2] *The Education Of Henry Adams* (The Modern Library, 1931), p. 385.

who have never been gentle in their habits. This is a situation which may so much discourage American negro leaders that they will abandon any effort at organized betterment.

Separatism could in the end prove easier for individuals who from childhood have been confronted by two codes of conduct, one within their own community and the other towards an incalculable if not actively unfriendly other world. Some negro leaders may sense that 'integration' or 'segregation' will come to the same thing: their race will never be anything more than shabby camp-followers and in conditions which hold out no promise of dignity is likely to become more rather than less animal. They will want to go their own way. And for the non-American world this will be the signal that 1776 has come to an end.

For the Americans the problem will still not be solved. Spasms of bad conscience by white Americans will result in half-removals of obstacles to integration and raise local hopes of revolt. Growing urban lawlessness and crime will encourage violent action among any group with a grievance: Black Power groups under one name or another will flourish ever and anon in the city jungles. And then the negro offers his own allurement as the purveyor of the lowest forms of indulgence so that those finding no more inspiration in Man can revert to the animal, not only the hippy and the obsessional but all those whose intuitions are blunted and bored, and there will be ever more of these.

North Americans are neither greedier nor more materialist than the rest of mankind. They are not to be attacked for having succeeded in doing better what the vast majority of the human race have aimed at. But nevertheless we have to ask: What next? Since U.S. governments desire and proclaim Western leadership and so many European politicians affect to desire and accept it, where shall we be led? The idealistic aspects of Marshall Aid and of the American challenge to Soviet policy in Europe were undoubted. But the Marshall Plan was used as a treacherous pressure weapon against Allies and the Cold War crusade turned into domestic McCarthyism. Even one of the farces of history repeated itself: Kennedy's 'Grand Design' for Europe finished like Roosevelt's New Deal in a dispute over plucked chickens.[3] There will always be action and reaction between American and European

[3] The National Recovery Act which was the basis of Federal economic powers under the 'New Deal' was declared unconstitutional by the Supreme Court in a case involving regulation of dressed poultry. The Grand Design hit the E.E.C. desire to protect its domestic market for the same product.

hopes and fears: for better or worse the external world will never permit the United States to lapse into a faceless Canada adjusting itself to a limited role.

Boyhood romances throw glamour and nobility over American causes and conflicts, and their Presidents—at least those whose names we can remember—have always seemed larger than life. So we tend to be disillusioned with their contemporary acts and Americans resent this unreasoning attitude, not always sensing that they are born of European self-resentment or of Utopian self-imagery which has not been realized in the cold hard world. The American responsibility for the outcome of some major international issue is thus often difficult to disentangle; Europe's political radicals, who are great Utopia inventors, have long ago decided to give the Russians the benefit of political doubt and use the United States as their hate object.

Unfortunately American self-consciousness adds some credence to the roles in which we cast them. They had always painted their own virtues in contrasting colours to the vices of the Old World and their present denigration of themselves fits in too aptly with the European Left's present projection of America. The love-hate relationship remains and, even worse, on the United States doorstep sits the perennial problem of Latin America. The higher the moral plane on which Washington puts its well-meaning interventions, the more these are resented. Latin America only teaches the lesson that emancipation from racial, ideological, and religious bonds fails to create Man. Throughout most of self-conscious mankind the forces which the United States wittingly or unwittingly released will be generally antagonistic to its policies.

The latest Western experiment of a global institutionalized Man —the United Nations—suffers from the same malady. In its first decade it appeared to progress because it met the needs of American power politics and could be manipulated by the United States Government. Our determination to project universals where there were only the particulars of what we called the 'Third World' sustained the illusion that here was a path to world government, although the self-consciousness of Africans and Asians must by its very nature result in divisive instinctual conflicts and the spread of modern technology is more likely to serve passion and aggression than reason. And from illusion was born error as Western politicians failed to distinguish—or sometimes chose not to distinguish—between popular movements struggling for independence and other forms of activism with designs on their neighbours: the result is that the risk of World War Three lies rather in the emotional and uncritical support given to the ambitions of small fry than in direct Great Power confrontations.

The maintenance of this mental confusion becomes a vested interest particularly among the placemen who conduct our diplomacy. And as the concepts of international law are cut off from their European origins they lose their attribute of law and become its opposite— arbitrariness. The concept of a legal personality which is generally conferred on any organization set up under treaty, such as the United Nations, and which is intended to bind it by obligation as much as to give it rights, is now proclaimed by Western 'progressive jurists' as being a law-making authority. Under this, aggression is called peaceful intent and terrorism becomes liberation, while 'rights' are for those who measure up to such double standards. When a concept becomes its opposite then it is time for its abandonment or overthrow.

The shortcomings of the United Nations have never derived from its newness nor from the immaturity of the majority of its members. To all of them the notion of impartiality, which underlies European jurisprudence and to some extent the older Islamic notions of law-making, is lacking and always will be because all are subject-centred, all are committed to the particular. The spread of 'knowledge' about each other will not change their attitudes. The Arabs are very well-informed indeed about Jews, their ways and their capabilities, as are Haussa about Ibo, and Somalis about Ethiopians: and the more they know about each other the sharper their attitudes become. A 'world institution' can only be a Western concept, run on Western lines: the very notion of an Arab, Chinese, or negro style of running world affairs should make us laugh: but it is precisely the rejection of the universality of Western institutions which characterizes the new mis-named national-isms. While non-alignment or neutrality are useful slogans for keeping out of Russo-American or Russo-Chinese disputes, the Africans and Asians will readily—with the aid of U Thant's Oriental cunning— harry those they believe are vulnerable.

Because liberal-humanists are not prepared to face this they would rather perpetuate the lie even if it destroys the whole European tradition of law. One further unfortunate consequence is that African and Asian political leaders, who are groping uncertainly in a 'world' which we created for them, have turned to what they believe is totali-tarianism as they find that the parliamentary system is patently inappli-cable to their own states: by insisting they shall have our system we open the way to the Communist alternative. And then in the belief that they are adopting a liberal stance to inevitability, the British and American governments have seemed to encourage the destruction of the European inheritance of law and contract. They have even supplied arms for massacre in Biafra when left to themselves the Africans might by palaver have produced their own symbiotic solution. The nation-state, born of our conscious formulations of privilege, will always sit un-easily on other ethnic and linguistic groupings. Reason does not require a choice between atrocities, as suggested by Mr. Peregrine Worsthorne,[4] but should not force choices where there is only instinctual continuum.

So when Portugal protests to the United States and Britain at their acquiescence in the Afro-Asian majority's twisting the Chapters and Articles of the U.N. Charter to suit the expediencies of daily debate, she is right to remind us of the dangers of destroying our own standards of criticism. Spain and Portugal are dismissed by Western liberals as unworthy of Europe, as if our claim on the future could be divorced from a past shared with Henry the Navigator, Vasco da Gama, Isabella and Ferdinand. The qualities of the *conquistadores* were only those of Hawkins and Drake. The preservation of what is distinctively European requires the rational recovery of the past as well as a sense of participation in the present. Without realizing it, Western Europe has reversed the whole process by which we have advanced from tribe to *Rechtsstaat*, and when the wretched British Monarch is obliged by her Ministers to stand up in Westminster and repeat her lesson that we should all become citizens of the world,[5] she is committing an act of betrayal as heinous as that of King Charles against those who trusted him: for her Coronation Oath requires her to maintain the laws and customs of the land. The legitimacy that must be at the end of the road back to loyalty will require a firm assertion by Western Europe that law stands above arbitrariness.

In the meantime more plausible propositions have become con-joined to the world institutions: Man has been indulging in narcissism in the form of philanthropy with its curious blend of self-flattery and guilt. If stern and thrifty Victorians saw the Irish potato famine largely as a divine visitation, we have become almost pathological in our dismissal of any evidence that World Banks, official aid, voluntary service and overseas famine relief have little practical outcome and

---

[4] 'The Atrocious Choice', *Sunday Telegraph*, 23.11.69.
[5] U.N. 25th Anniversary Celebration in Westminster Hall.

resolutely refuse to accept Indian indifference to individual human fate
or Pakistani self-centredness as decisive factors in economic life.

While Europeans may need to bolster up their identity with
occasional demonstrations of altruism, it is by no means proven that
civic virtue is developed in proportion to the intensity and frequency
of this. Nor does the corollary stand, that our society will become more
selfish if we do not continually applaud benevolence in others. Moods
of guilt, self-righteousness, or benevolence are unreliable guides when
society as a whole is called upon to participate as an act of policy. A
rational case for aid depends on there being a world where rationality
is an effective factor. The American disillusionment after twenty years
of foreign-aid programmes has resulted in a general scepticism—'a
fatigue bordering on sleeping sickness' as one aid administrator has
put it—without any fundamental re-examination of the policy because
this would mean questioning fundamentals about Man himself, admitting the Old Adam with the old arguments about the inability to
change human nature, recognition of the uniqueness of Western ways
and of the unwillingness of Africa and Asia to accept change, the
rejection in fact of President Kennedy's proposition in 1963 that 'aid
serves our own national traditions as well as our national interests'.

Even the oft-repeated view that the world is *now* economically
interdependent and therefore requires a global aid programme is
meaningless. For the 'world' has always been interdependent—the
silk of China, the ivory of India, the sultanas of Turkey, the wheat of
the Baltic, and wines of Gascony found their way over the trade routes
and the oldest excavations of human settlement reveal instruments and
tools from far and near. The Western world has become conscious of
this: but there is no indication that the Third World is prepared to
abandon its own satisfactions in order to support the economic hypo-
theses of professional aid-givers. The probable consequences of feeding
and clothing others in our own image has to be submitted to the same
rational tests as ruling or taxing them. And when we find that the
same names which are associated with campaigns of denunciation are
figuring in the benevolent appeals, it is time to beware. Narcissus
wants to be thought well of: he is not thinking well of others.

It seems easier to stumble in and out of empire than to adjust our
thoughts first to the sort of responsibilities we have assumed and then,
when the empire has vanished, to disentangle our thoughts from our
imperial self-image. The easy way out has been to persist in the pretence
of a Commonwealth 'club' with its jargon about admission, member-

ship, traditions, and expulsion. It is all so unique, we claim. It is of course nothing of the sort. It is a latter-day equivalent of the Holy Roman Empire in its last shadowy century, still with an Imperial chancery and a nominal postal service, courts which arbitrated on irrelevant matters, and ever more elaborate protocol for the occasional electoral assemblies. 'Das heilige römische Reich, wie hält es sich zusammen?' sang the revellers in Auerbach's cellar; in practice it had already fallen apart. Similarly in the sixties the aged Attlee used to totter to his feet to point at the red on the out-of-date maps which always seem to hang on the walls of our learned societies and exclaim: 'Can we abandon all this?' 'This' had abandoned us long ago. Yet in 1970 Lord Butler was announcing at a Press conference in New Delhi: 'England should be a centre for the world, not just for itself!' He then called for '. . . a healthy number of Indians and Pakistanis to come in'.[6] It was again Mr. Enoch Powell who had to enunciate the unspeakable: 'The great majority of people in this country . . . would be very happy to see the end of this humbug of the Commonwealth.'[7]

The irrational basis of all this is emphasized by the fact that it is the British and Dutch who have the most tender conscience about the lands and peoples over which they once ruled. Their administrations over the last half-century of colonialism were characterized by genuine self-sacrifice and devotion to the advancement of the local peoples. The Latin races, who permitted the continuation of practices in their overseas territories which we jettisoned with the demise of the John Company, are neither plagued by such inner prickings nor thought one whit the worse by their former colonial subjects on that account. The tangled skein of human history cannot be cut up into pieces labelled good and evil.

The backward look into empire with all its triumphs, cruelties, and misunderstandings only tells the same tangled tale of all mankind. It does not provide justification for a mood of guilt, nor for indulgence in nostalgia. If the *raj* was in practice the export of suburbia, so to-day's 'world problems' such as Viet-Nam, Cuba, the Middle East, are local issues with which we have allowed ourselves to become obsessed and where we have over-estimated our capacity to influence the outcome. Our Eurocentrism causes us to see 'regions' such as South-East Asia, imagining that geographical proximity can lead to common rational

[6] 16.3.70.
[7] B.B.C. broadcast, 26.10.70.

solutions. We can spot fallacies in Russian arguments as to why world Communism must ultimately triumph. We are less successful in spotting our own. Laotians, Cambodians, Vietnamese, Somalis, Kikuyu, and Congolese may not fit into Marxist categories: but neither will they permit themselves to be forced into a European mould of regionalism.

African and Asian alignments and alliances will be determined by their feeling for immediate advantage. This may result in their mortgaging their economic resources for arms but on the other hand intrigue and the immediate satisfaction of greed may ensure that essential moment of stability for a ruler to consolidate his power. Since those who live by mood have the highest degree of sensitivity to the mood of fear in others, fear will be their main instrument of rule. And if they sense it among Europeans, they will be after us too. The unity of mankind which would then be created would be that of the basic jackal. Fear therefore is the one thing which Europe must never show in the face of Africa and Asia and if we have read our history aright it is the last thing we need ever have any cause to show. Britain in particular should by now have seen that she has neither gained credit nor increased by one iota her influence in Asia and Africa by her policy of accommodation to their extravaganzas. The time for the betrayal of Europe by Europeans is over.

The communities of European settlement throughout the world have also developed their self-conscious identities. If some of their present policies, such as 'White Australia' or South Africa's separate communal development, clash with to-day's monolithic morality of Man, they will mean something very different in to-morrow's world of diversity. The creation of chaos in such territories will solve nothing: their preservation as active centres may serve in future decades as new bases for outward creation. The dying cultures of mankind, such as the Celtic, bear witness to past failures to preserve such centres in a world of intrusion and violence.

And a comparison of the forms of consciousness reached through human divergence and diversity offers the possibility of a new concept of mankind, one which will enable us to recast our political concepts in a new time-scale and refute the dogmatic finalities of the ideologues of yesteryear posing as this season's progressives. If we still wish to use the two old metaphysical *a priori* concepts of the study of consciousness—Being and Knowing—we can rediscover the former as the transition of moods through which all mankind has passed and is still passing to new stages of self-consciousness. Western 'Knowing' has been the growth of temporal formulation expressed in rational concepts of causality. The cunning or *Kunst* which the Western world now treats as an inferior method still finds favour with the rest of mankind as *the* human wisdom. For them 'Being' remains an intuition and in most non-European tongues the relationship between actions is more important than the position of the actions in time. Distinctions which we regard as of time may with other peoples be aspects of space, while the Arab rightly calls his conjugation *haraka*—movement. In other linguistic traditions one word can reflect several aspects—duration, inception, and participation—so that utterance reflects the fluidity of thought and action as against the Western hypostasized conventions of language which give our ideas the illusion of being handy objects. We recognize the cunning which exploits the immediacy of actions but are irritated that it eludes our definitions. So we are always calling the Arabs liars when in practice they have never been concerned with true or false statements. With Africans and Hopi Indians we may not even be able to agree that the grass is green. For the former it is yellow and with the latter the colour depends on the position of the sun. For language is never a 'fact', never the existent singular of the philosopher's definition. To seek for resemblances and reconciliations between facts instead of accepting the different emphases of action leaves us trapped with the sterile universals which breed betrayal.

Whether men have come to look for similarities or differences in objects has depended on myriad needs of family and tribe, on the impact of environment during the long process of disengaging consciousness of self, and doubtless on genetic factors which operated in different degrees with different men and whose legacy is still with us even if the setting in which they originally functioned is not. The common general factor of self-consciousness has meant that in some degree all men have transferred the qualities of objects back on to themselves and given them 'human' attributes. But whether the notion and name of the object and any subsequent mental creations acquired an appearance of complete autonomy has depended on how far the subject, after first gaining a precarious sense of identity, has abstracted himself from his environment. This last has been the gift of temporal rationality. By providing the strongest sense of permanence in the midst of changing circumstances, it confers the widest range of freedom within which thought can range and gives European man his claim on privilege.

The groups of mankind whose thought has remained part of a continuum, whose speech has retained its immediacy, and who have not ventured to transmute emotive utterance into denotative, have no such claim. But they enjoy another form of security, they are left with greater human warmth, with the capacity for indulgence without guilt, with perhaps a keener sense for the qualities of things and relations. The risk to us is that when we fear for our identity, we reattach ourselves not to a human continuum but to words now become brittle inhuman objects. European rationality is still precariously suspended between time and mood: its fragility is its uniqueness. We shall find it nowhere else and wherever we search—among Samoans and Eskimos—we shall merely find that while all men are imitative and curious tool-users, they have achieved such a rich diversity of societies that an identity of Man can be ruled out. At most we can reflect that if we had never adopted the image of the *allgemein-menschliches* but, like the Eskimo in his hunting days imitating the seal's habits, remained completely attuned to the rhythms of external phenomena, we should not now be coping with the problems of a too highly developed self-consciousness. This also means that since we cannot make our own past, present, and future a common possession, our contemporary insights can never be the common assumptions of a generalized wisdom of mankind.

What then is the next step? We can share some human insights with the African when we are with him in immediate human situations: we can calculate at the price of some rather ambiguous face-saving our common material self-interest with Asians. With the Russians we can argue out rationally if slowly and painfully some joint common assumptions on how to avoid mutual destruction. We can be sufficiently strong to warn off the Americans if in their search for a new myth of identity they should again threaten our kith and kin. For no one can say how long present power alignments may last. The aftermath of John Foster Dulles' death found the Germans swinging in slightly hysterical fashion between France and the United States as if in search of a leader: the attraction of power is still central to loyalty. The question mark that suddenly appeared over the world after the Dallas murder illustrated how dependent we all had become on the random elements of American domestic politics and underlined the need for Europeans to be able to appraise their own role. If Washington's need to appease its negro minority committed it further to supporting black racial aggression in Africa, or if the coarsening process of American society brought about some wild crisis of uncertainty, Europe would have to make its own stand against spreading world chaos or go under. Such an eventuality may never arise. The United States may yet find a new secure identity and also reject irrational Man in favour of a rational acceptance of human diversity. But a major factor in bringing Americans to such a recognition will be a European assertion: in dark or uncertain ages men have first to establish their own privileges before later generations can sustain their legitimacy.

If the old maps are put away and we look afresh at the world of self-conscious human diversity, it is possible to see outlines emerging from the post-1945 decades with their overtones of wartime alliances and ideological conflicts. Like the peasants and sutlers of northern France hesitatingly approaching the Viking camps to offer their goods, we can test reality by a calculation of risk and gain. If we cease to regard Africa and Asia as moral cheering squads in our games of power or in our schemes for world government, we shall see that they bear a resemblance, and more than a superficial one, to worlds that older venturers such as the Ottoman Turks, Venetians, Genoese, and eventually the Western seaboard peoples knew well as they followed their paths of conquest and trade. Two hundred years of European imperial and colonial rule have not changed mankind: they have given it a sharper sense of identity.

Yet the emancipation of the racial communities of the Ottoman Empire did not result in a settled mosaic of nation-states in the European sense, nor could the French and British mandatory powers during their interlude play the same role as the *dowlah*. The former subject peoples still needed to participate in a wider drama where action and intuition played a lead and their consciousness required something to fill the gap. This could not be a rational imposition because the peoples had not taken part in the evolution of the concept of temporal rationality. Arab emotions found a substitute in an Arab 'unity' which has never been realized, and probably never will be, and can only be credible while there is an enemy. But it is still the ghost of the *dowlah* which haunts the Arabs as once legends of 'Rum' lingered in Turkish memories.

Similarly, the era of European power domination created forms of participation which will never entirely vanish and will leave Asians and Africans with some vague hunger or need for their identity to be linked with a larger one, of what kind they know not themselves. The end of empire bequeaths the fear of being random: perhaps it was because of this that in the Dark Ages European rulers and subjects so eagerly sought legitimacy in the revival of the concepts of Rome. To-day we are in all likelihood faced with a long era where there will be an ill-defined legacy of European ascendancy, a need among non-European peoples for an impartiality which only Europeans can provide, but still a world of aimless revolts and conflicts where our intervention may still be called upon. There will be continuing paradoxes as in the Middle East where the unmentionable in the form of well-equipped Israeli forces is the main factor in creating the unheard-of, namely Arab restraint. There could be other situations where the European capacity to exercise a *de facto* authority will be more important than the observance of formal legitimacy. It will be the sort of world where once Europeans—formerly dubbed 'mercenaries', now labelled 'expatriates'—drilled outlandish armies, cast cannon for their rulers, and organized their finance and their commerce, where there will doubtless be corruption and violence, but also risk and adventure. Europe through various forms of co-operation will still be able to offer participation provided it retains its own identity.

But owing to the confusion of first- and second-order factors, Europeans are not only in danger of losing the sense of what is distinctively European, but have become afraid of new forms: the universal seems to exclude them. If Europe's role for a long period involves coping with a variety of separate assertive identities and at the same time trying to satisfy their need for participation, we shall have to face political forms and relationships which have no precedents. Yet it has been the willingness to adventure which has made the European a creator. The other agents to which academic writers now give such emphasis—economic forces and technical and scientific discovery—have played their unique role in Western history because of the direction given to them by the European conceptualizing mind: even natural disaster was turned to advantage. In other civilizations there has been no such consequence.[8] By being himself *auctor* the European has made himself his own authority.

[8] In a B.B.C. External Broadcast for New Year 1970, entitled 'Into The Seventies', the Indian writer V. S. Naipaul said: 'In the more static cultures —those primarily of the underdeveloped countries—the mind is more or less at rest. It is this intellectual gap which I find more disturbing than the technological gap. I think even as the world is, it can be divided into the inferior—those societies that are totally inferior—and those that are always moving, always progressing, whose more gifted members are always working at the frontiers, in whatever field. I see the future as rather horrible. But not, I think, for the rich countries. Only for the poor. And they have so little thought at the moment that I don't think they will be excessively distressed. This distress will be in the mind of the observer.'

So it would seem that although we ourselves can create rational assumptions about all men, we cannot do so for them. The instinctive-subjective world of Further Asia cannot sustain the scientific-objective order created by the West. The Arab world of emotional satisfactions can create no abiding concepts of state and society. Other societies lack even the capacity to maintain themselves in the contemporary world. And our schemes for world government ignore our own whole trend of critical reasoning, that there can never be an absolute or final authority. The world authority is expected to take care of the prevention of global nuclear war, the control of disarmament, keeping the peace, and advancing material and spiritual welfare. We are not even agreed how or whether our own governments should concern themselves with all these matters. 'Weltkunde ausgezeichnet. Heimatkunde schwach', as the old Prussian school reports used to say.

Authority, like all human institutions, grows out of a need. 'Every constitution must first gain authority and then use authority: it must first win the loyalty and confidence of mankind and then employ that homage in the work of government', wrote Bagehot. But there have been many needs and for each an authority has to be invoked. In a country's domestic affairs we accept such a plurality and if we grant to State authority an overriding legitimacy in the use of force in certain situations, this is because we recognized that in reasonably peaceable societies other types of force were no longer required or even desirable. There is thus a well-defined historical context for the legitimacy of the authority which controls relationships of power with other states. But the authority which can impose notions requires another justification while the authority which can give us a sense of well-being is of a different order entirely. So in the acceptance of human diversity there must be a plurality: there will be no assurance of identity if one half of mankind is continually under threat from the other half. Order in the world will never be identical with a world order.

When the destructive elements of our own society allege that after Hitler we cannot claim virtue for Europe against other continents or groupings of mankind, this argument need only be stood on its head. For the rise of Naziism can be read as a lesson to insist on the rigorous maintenance of our own standards and to prevent the spread of the 'anything goes' atmosphere of the Weimar Republic which by 1933 made Hitler seem little more unappealing than other choices. The process of togetherness through debasement will lead sooner or later to a similar predicament; for the best of us will do things in groups which

M

we should never have dreamt of as individuals, and at the lowest level it will be the psychopath who will be the focus of group loyalties. Group cults of action and violence without aim will result in a relapse into mood. With our present inversion the temptation is stronger than ever before. Long before Proust saw men breaking under the load of time, Descartes wrote of the 'terror of a failure in time'.

If the mood of the present were to overcome the remembrance of things past that would be the end of our history, a true return to barbarism. Like the Bedouin we would stand in wonder before the Sabatean and Nabatean ruins and inscriptions exclaiming that they were the work of genii or of ancient giants, not realizing that they were the creations of our fathers and the language was our own. Although the material achievements of civilization can sometimes be reconstructed when the remembrance of it is there, a lost sense of time will not be recovered.

Faust indeed symbolizes our predicament of being torn between the immediacy of experience and the demands of time. For although we try to sustain the sense of an inner duration by reassessing the effects of successive changes in new concepts, our consciousness of existence still depends on the present. The needs of the moment with their intuitive references and relationships continually clash with our intellectual reconciliations, particularly those of religion and philosophy. Memory alone, which is not time, can mislead us. Turning back on ourselves seems a comfortable refuge and perhaps the English have been trying to live thus, communing with the dream lives of others by myths and older affective modes of communication. Others who abandon their Faustian role go off to play Don Quixote and try to impose their inner dreams on some unlikely external reality. But since our society is detribalized, disintegrated, and increasingly mechanized, an inner-directed lonely crowd is most likely to succumb to fear—the strongest emotion of all and the characteristic of barbarian societies.

When a society is increasingly uncertain as to its basic assumptions and loyalties and individuals are withdrawing on themselves, large-scale alien intrusions become doubly disintegrative. Historians can argue in contemporary terms whether the irruption of the Syrian flute-players brought about improvement or deterioration in Roman life. At the time some Romans had definite views: they sensed clearly enough as their society became less homogeneous that there were fewer agreed assumptions as to conduct and that dissolution was taking place. And now Britain faces intrusions on a scale and of a type which could within a decade break up the whole structure of society. For a whole assortment of diverse assertive humanity has been allowed to flood in on a scale which makes any form of assimilation impossible.

The protagonists of multi-racialism find pride in the prospect of Britain becoming what they term a microcosm of the world. And so it may become, as our national institutions break up like the United Nations under the burden of incompatibilities and our own laws become arbitrary. Citizenship and nationality are no longer determined by individual allegiance but by arbitrary categories: the Race Relations Acts deliberately set out to destroy the preferences of Scots and English for each other's company or services. As more and more police powers are invoked in what should be the field of normal personal choice, observance of law is replaced by a hide-and-seek between enforcement and evasion. The basis of the 'Welfare State', namely the monogamous family with responsible parents, is incompatible with the acceptance of Moslem polygamy and changing West Indian liaisons: protection of minors and Hindu child marriage prove irreconcilable.

The destructive elements of our own society—all those who have never been able for one reason or another to identify themselves with it—welcome this development. They are least of all likely to permit what will be the only peaceful solution to the problem created by the influx of two million immigrants of other cultures or of no-cultures, namely mass repatriation. And since the destructive elements largely dominate the daily media of communication, they could delay solution until violence had taken over: they may be even found excusing the violence in its early stages.[9]

---

[9] 'Into a normal situation inject a new element of purposeless violence and aggression: quite a little violence will do for a start, and quite a few individuals are sufficient to begin with. Everyone is startled and astonished. Suddenly news exists where there was none before—pictures, action, reports. As the violence was purposeless, everybody is bound to set to work at once on discovering its purpose.

'This sort of stuff is irresistibly tempting to the liberals and reformers who are soon, in various degrees, heard condemning what is called "repression", condoning violence, explaining it away, and sometimes all but calling for more of it.

'What an extraordinary result: so much from so little—almost from nothing. A simple technique, simplicity itself: yet it has all but destroyed governments and states in Asia, in Europe and in America. It is at work at this moment in a part of the United Kingdom.'

Enoch Powell. Speech at Wolverhampton Conservative Association, 28.8.69. His reference to 'a part of the United Kingdom' was to Ulster.

Because of this, if violence does come, it will take some of the aspects of a civil war, from which a new sense of allegiance may painfully be born. But even if we avoid this, physical disengagement from other races is as essential for our survival as is a rational reassessment of our relations with them in their own lands. The fabric of society no longer rests on the unselfconscious assumptions of common traditions nor on the ready interchangeability of instinctive habits while, because of our inversion, the rational framework is in a fragile state. Sizeable non-European intrusions which bring about a lowering rather than a raising of common denominators will only mean growing psychopathic outbreaks in our urban jungles. And when the aqueducts have finally fallen into disrepair and the temples have been abandoned to strange cults or become dumping grounds for uncollected garbage, no one will remember how it came about.

So the British, like other peoples, have also a particular identity to preserve, while the legitimacy and the authority which beckon at the end of the road back to loyalty are the concepts of European history. But the concepts must never become monolithic. They must allow for the human intuitive elements which have also combined to form our historical identity. If Equality becomes a pure institution, men become interchangeable pawns; if Liberty becomes absolute, our liberties perish; the Universal eliminates the human. So Monsignor Montini was not an exception, only rather more obvious.

The monolithic betrayals are not inevitable. Our bodies have evolved to cope with physical diversity: our mental evolution is certainly not otherwise. So in place of Man, Morality, Equality and God, we can set about rediscovering men, moralities, and even gods who can hold our particular allegiances. For the Greek pantheon helps us to cope with the sudden challenges of the moment. It is the essence of the present that many things are happening, many of which appear irrelevant to each other. We can cope with this diversity. 'The occasion arises from relevant objects and perishes into the status of an object. But it enjoys its decisive moment of absolute self-attainment as an emotional unity.'[10] If through change and stress men can share this unity, loyalty will be preserved.

[10] Whitehead, *Adventures of Ideas,* p. 179.

VIII. Style and Purpose

VIII. Style and Purpose

The loyalties of the people are there: they await only a new focus. No substitute of function, interest, or contrived communication can meet their need: the restoration of emotional unity requires a new sense of communal action and since our whole body of ideas is involved, it is from above that new initiatives must come. Mr. Edward Heath spoke better than he knew when he offered a new style of government. This must be part of the process by which the individual recovers assurance in the midst of accelerating change in environment, work, and associations. Since Labour's identity tags are tied to the universalist ideas which have brought betrayal and in our time treason bears a Left-Wing label, only a Conservative Government can play this role.

However risky it may be to hail a contemporary event as a turning point, the General Election result of 1970 did signify more than the replacement of one set of Jacks-in-office by another. By the spring of 1970 those who affected to interpret the moods of the British nation were unanimous that Labour would be re-elected and that six years of Wilson had in some way sapped the will of the electorate to bring about change.[1] Did the surprise reversal support the theory that an election turn-round comes about when the bulk of the nation moves defensively, sensing that its material interests are threatened, and at the same time party activists are sufficiently stirred by non-material considerations at home and abroad—'an idea to admire and an ideology to hate', as has been said—to put in that enthusiastic effort which can be the determining marginal factor in victory?[2]

Something more than even that has happened. The departure of

[1] In 'What Kind of Country?' (*Sunday Telegraph*, 14.6.70) Peregrine Worsthorne advanced the view that Labour rule 'creates conditions which guarantee its continuity, since the country can no longer summon up the will to escape'.
[2] This theory, advanced by Trevor Lloyd in *The General Election of 1880*, receives up-to-date discussion by Robert Blake in *The Conservative Party: From Peel to Churchill* (Eyre & Spottiswoode, 1970), pp. 266–8.

Sir Edward (now Lord) Boyle and the death of Mr. Iain Macleod symbolized the end of the consensus politics by which issues of national importance were evaded under cover of philanthropic universalizing. The slow inward change in the Conservative Party had been unmistakably heralded when the unbelievable occurred and at the annual Party conference in 1969 a Tory leader, in the shape of Mr. Quintin Hogg, was booed and hissed. A large section of the electorate is no longer being taken in by affective associations of ideas, whatever intrigues and deceptions may still continue among the politicians themselves in their internal jockeyings for office. It may be that we have come to the end of the style of politics as conducted by Lloyd George. One day we had to grow out of it and perhaps that day has come. We shall only be certain if we see political ideas emerging which are accurate descriptions of human motivation. When this does happen it will be fatal to the Old and New Left whose demagogic appeal centres round the theme of 'Man'.

But the first hurdles facing those who take office are inevitably the practical consequences bequeathed by their predecessors. If democracy could not have survived another battering of the kind suffered under Labour, neither will it survive in its present form, according to Lord Shawcross, if at the end of its five-year term the present Government has not put the country back on the road to economic progress and stability.[3] What rate of progress and what degree of stability are doubtless arguable! But it is more than likely that, if in two or three years government leaders are still believed to be running after events instead of mastering and controlling them, the disintegrating and violent elements in society will have become relatively stronger. Authority has to be seen to be effective and even more clearly be seen to be reducing arbitrariness, not increasing it.

In a nation which has hitherto mainly responded intuitively to historical symbols now, like the Crown, somewhat discredited, selecting the principles of action will not be easy. Nowhere is this more obvious than over industrial relations which the Conservatives chose to pick up as their first challenge. On the surface here is arbitrariness crying to be brought within a framework of law. Yet the apparent arbitrary conduct of 'unofficial' strikers reflects a change which cannot be reversed. Even if this has been exploited by ambitious men in ways which damage society, the solution cannot be by penalty alone. It

[3] Speech to Birmingham Chamber of Commerce, 25.11.70.

has taken many decades for the formal democratic 'rights' of last century to become effective democratization in industrial affairs but this has happened. Trade unionists no longer accept decisions handed down by an élite; a better level of education, new ranges of occupational experience in a more technically sophisticated setting, have given them a sense of economic competence and political power. This may at times be misused but there are now human forces which need guidance and not repression.

But the trade unionist is also citizen, consumer, and saver, and so has other stakes in the proper functioning of society. He is open to other arguments, to observe agreements and contracts on the basis that he is hurting his other self, particularly when the public reacts strongly against strike actions which cause it inconvenience and hardship. So the new laws must be shown to be part of a larger communal action from which all can benefit. The new style of leadership must be ready with a new statement of general ideas on the organization of society.

The same kind of issue is being forced upon us by a second major economic factor. The industrialized nations of the Western world are approaching a point where they can offer their members a livelihood within a gradually diminishing working day or week. The recognition that a man's existence is no longer determined by a twenty-four-hour necessity from which free time has to be snatched, implies a new concept of occupation itself. The problem has emerged in the United States in the form of a standing army of unemployed on relief, while for many of those in employment 'leisure' has become boredom to be dispelled by artifices which create only more boredom. Since in Europe there is no great mass of unskilled and largely unemployed negro labour, the first part of the American dilemma is not likely to be duplicated but the second will be—that of finding use for a 'leisure' which is not of choice but at times virtually an enforcement. In British industry over-manning and restrictive practices have up to now been the by-product: but these too have ceased to be even a delaying tactic in the face of narrowing profit margins for present and future investment. The issue can no longer be evaded.

Yet this could be the development which would bring a greater spirit of objectivity back into our society and enable individuals to welcome change and profit from it, instead of resenting it or fighting against it. If our days of unconscious and instinctive assumptions are over, the logical step is to open up to individuals fresh perspectives of conscious decision so that they can step out of any mode of life which no longer satisfies them into one which offers them new personal and social roles. Stepping on a new shore opens up new horizons to the emigrant, imparts a new feeling of independence, the need to reject old received values and formulate his own: it is his confidence in his new-found capacities which sets the style of his society. And this we can now effect at home by encouraging the notion of a second occupation and by ensuring that the means for furthering it are made available to those who seek the opportunity. On a modest scale this is already practised as 'redundancy training'. Sweden accepts it as an essential element of the process of modernizing and remanning industry. It can be made a general pattern of society.

No doubt the majority will prefer to continue to occupy themselves in one groove of life and outside working hours prefer idleness or escapism. Their family may absorb them or their first occupation may have provided them with a true vocation. But for the enterprising and the ambitious, the prospect should be open to facilitate a fresh start into a new life sufficiently different from the old for the individual to be able, in course of time, to look back to the man he once was and savour the realization of some of his dreams. This is not a mere question of helping women and men to swap jobs but through changes in our whole educational, professional, economic, and social framework to bring about the general recognition that no man need be tied for life to one treadmill.

Given an increasing number of women and men who have given their lives a new conscious direction, a new experienced tone can be struck in society. Many of them may make a straight change between skills: all of them will bring some form of reflective judgement to bear on their old lives and some conscious resolutions for the new. For the individual this means that motivation and rationalization can be brought together, that he can feel he is the master and not the victim of change, and that change can reinforce and not undermine identity. If instead of living an inner fantasy life a man reaches for a new outward one he will have a better sense that *he* is the source of emotion and not be misled by the transfer of emotions to the object: no longer like the child hitting back at the object which has hurt him, he will now know how to bring it under his creative control. Will this make men less susceptible to fraudulent associations of ideas and to the manufactured personalities at present foisted on them and which ultimately degrade them? The stifling of the urge to aspire affects most of all the sensitive fringe which supplies thinkers, pioneers, and discoverers: but in a society which offers individuals the opportunity to realize the foiled aspirations of earlier days, a transition from inversion to the realization of one's life as an objective creation may produce as remarkable an outburst as the older European physical thrust outwards into the world. In the transitive society new loyalty will be found.

But how is this to be brought about? A new structure of society can never be imposed: it can only be sustained if it grows out of the interplay of existing human desires and satisfactions and can hold out the promise of increasing resources and new material rewards. Existing 'vested interests' have either to be dispersed or conciliated. Although industrial and scientific diversification is increasingly bringing new men to the top, society is still basically an age pyramid with skills becoming scarcer as men grow older, so that in the administrative hierarchy of business and government, the senior jobs still fall mainly to the elderly. The switches between professions as conducted at present aggravate our state rather than ameliorate it. Generally these take place after retirement in one profession or at such a late age that the rigid myths of incipient senility are merely transferred to another sphere. The tall amiable ones, who know how to make treachery palatable, are most skilful in blocking change, smothering issues, and bear a major responsibility for the lack of fresh definitions of human purpose. The closed corporations of Westminster and Whitehall affect one standard, the outside world assumes another and within the corporation little self-images have built up their defensive outworks of self-preservation. The Prime Minister flatters himself on his skill in evasion so that the same art is practised on him. The learned judge at the Profumo inquiry could only suggest that the right questions had not been put: the reason that they were not is that the answers would have threatened the corporation's survival. Stratification persists where it is least desirable.

In practice the corporation is no more necessary to-day than it ever has been. The collection and dispensing of revenue, the running of courts of law, the equipment, direction, and planning of the armed forces—these three functions of central government are the only ones for which a permanent corps of specialist officials is essential. For all the rest, change is both possible and desirable, as 'temporaries' in war and peace have soon realized. So the Conservative intention of hiving off functions of state which they consider are the responsibility of the private sector must be extended to being a broad avenue of no-return, so that no future government can reverse the process save at the risk of arousing the widespread hostility of those who have had new perspectives opened up for them by a widened private sector.

And since the 'Welfare State' has come up against the limits of the British gross national product without solving problems of poverty, housing, saving, quality of education, and morality, the Tories are right to change course and call for a return to personal effort, individual conscience, and self-respect. Here too are vested interests to be overcome for which not all those involved are to blame, such as the working-class families who are prisoners in both jobs and council houses and who would lose roof and subsidy if they moved elsewhere. But as the welfare system goes beyond our administrative skill and capacity to maintain, it is starting to break up and the practical alternative can and must be found.[4]

It is one of the oldest arts in government that when a particular political issue becomes hazardous, it is swept up into a larger policy question. The redeployment and dismantling of the official bodies, laws, and practices which constitute the welfare services will have to be seen to be part of a policy by which flexibility, mobility, and transfer are encouraged throughout the whole structure of employment and professional activity; one which is opening up to the aggressive and the sensitive new opportunities for the purposeful reshaping of their lives and careers. This has to be a policy based on endowment, competition, bonus, bursary, and reward, and not on hand-out: it will be the test of whether Mr. Edward Heath is right in assuming that the individual wishes to take responsibility. But until mobility has added its own stimulus to social and economic change, the political system itself is not likely to improve greatly in quality: the participants in the political process—whether politicians or civil servants—will still find it only too easy to mask their cumulative failures behind universalizing platitudes, and in the seventies we shall still have parliamentary dinosaurs left over from the era when all the Fabians were young, putting answers of the thirties to questions which still date from the twenties.

Such a policy requires the open rejection of human equality, that principle to which all have paid lip service since Condorcet—unfor-

---

[4] Since this is not a book on the organization of state welfare services, I can do no more here than draw attention to *Down With The Poor*, ed. Dr. Rhodes-Boyson (Churchill Press, 1971). This is a penetrating analysis of the 'Welfare State' backed up by telling statistical material which puts forward an alternative method of organizing social services in a prosperous democracy.

tunately only guillotined after he had enunciated it—and in which nobody has ever believed. The whole course of economic legislation over the last hundred years has assumed that equality could be enforced and inequality swept under the rug. But the effort failed because it could never be an onslaught on inequality itself but only on those who for one reason or another were in a position to enjoy it. Like the tomb robbers of Ancient Egypt who were always one move ahead of the grave diggers, they have found new and ingenious ways of getting away with the booty. In the end inequality remains and the distressed are still with us although by cataloguing their distress we have eased our consciences and created, as Mr. Ralph Harris puts it, that strange race of sociologists who look as if they had done rather well out of the poor.[5]

The rejection of equality does not imply the imposition of inequality but the acceptance of diversity which involves emulation and encourages men to aim at excellence. Style, with which equality can dispense, becomes a need. If the concept of human diversity rejects Man, this does not mean the end of humanism, the essence of which, as suggested by H. J. Blackham, would appear to be that all men should be free to introduce their own purposes and multiply the possibilities of purpose by exploring the uses of things.[6] This may be as close as one can get to a definition of human progress. It means a leap into the unknown and the unexpected but it is precisely these which provide new knowledge, not the known and the inevitable. The European can cope with them: the tenses of his languages permit him the longer reaction time which brings the greatest gain in information and increases in turn the diversity of his knowledge.

To achieve this there will have to be a fundamental reshaping of the educational system, the scrapping of the present notions of straight quantitative expansion of schools and higher institutions, and a reassignment of the tasks of the last. Our formal systems for acquiring knowledge may even have to be reversed, starting from the basis of 'cunning', i.e. of learning a skill, and only after this has been acquired for work or profession, moving on to learning about 'knowing'. The present student troubles illustrate only too well the error of confronting young people suffering from the emotional instability which comes from the earlier onset of puberty with the problems of grappling with general

[5] 'Return To Reality', B.B.C. talk, 27.1.68.
[6] H. J. Blackham, *Political Discipline In A Free Society* (Allen and Unwin, 1961), p. 131.

concepts of human purpose before they have had the experience of adult motivation. The outcome is a prolongation of childhood games of 'good yins' and 'bad yins' projected on to issues which are sufficiently remote from practical daily preoccupations to be treated in terms of fantasy. All this has been grist to the mills of dons whose own immaturity has been prolonged within Oxbridge cloisters and Redbrick canteens and who through error or design describe infantile tantrums as moral sensitivity and pass off any form of authority as repression.

If the criteria of scholarship are being abandoned in undergraduate arts and social-science courses, there is a compelling case for dispensing with them altogether and leaving such subjects for mature students and post-graduates. Forms of knowledge, which in previous centuries required learned doctors and attentive pupils in continuous communication, can be acquired readily by those with sufficient experience of life to relate what they read and hear to what they see and do. 'The true university of these days is a library of books', said Carlyle so long ago that he has been forgotten: but the proposition remains true. The straight expansion of universities, the system of student grants which has created demand to the point where the genuine scholar suffers, and the lowered standards of teaching point nowhere except to disintegration. The process can be reversed by the straight imposition of higher standards of entry, and by the transfer of a large number of undergraduate schools to teachers' colleges and professional bodies. The new role of the university will be to assist those who come for their second occupation or for true higher study.

The reputation of European universities as centres of discovery and enlightened research rests on the interlude from mid-nineteenth century until early twentieth, when they possessed laboratory and library facilities superior to those of specialist or industrial establishments and for a few decades were in the scientific vanguard. But for most of their history they have been defenders of old shibboleths rather than pioneers in thought. Nor have they ever been zealous defenders of freedom of expression although they may have asserted this when claiming special privilege for their members. Over the last two hundred years, among all the university professors of Britain it is hard to think of even two dozen names which can be ranked in the highest category of original thinkers. Although self-conscious coteries and cliques build up their own cults which they try to pass off to the outside world as 'the cultivation of intellectual excellence', the primary duty of a university is, as it always has been, to teach and there is every indication that our universities are failing even in this. 'Wisdom' itself is derived from human experience, as it always has been.

If we can look to a wide exchange of experience between work bench, laboratory, profession, and schoolroom we can hope for the spreading of vigour and maturity throughout all walks of life and perhaps even the emergence of a new establishment, which will fill the vacuum left when the Edwardian one of grandees, admirals, and generals passed away. 'The Englishman is a king in a plain coat', said Emerson. Even as one of the outsiders (for Emerson deliberately excluded the Scots!) I heartily agree! If the king could enjoy his own again, society might recover some of the *gravitas* of communities where reflective men, from shepherd and blacksmith to employer and political aspirant, drawing from their careful reading and their experience of toil, gave quality back to the style of life. As it is, in spite of the attempts at subliminal denigration—as it has been called—of the British middle classes, their standards and habits still prevail and are shared by the aspiring elements of the working class. The great mass of the young are totally unlike the image of 'youth culture' promoted by the commercial exploiters of the riff-raff of the big cities.

Style to-day is treated as identical with fashion, but in truth it should be the outward indication of the communal sense of the fitting. Like religion and law, style should bind: it should express an ordering principle and there has been no great age of civilization which did not have a distinct sense of style accepted by its members as readily and as naturally as they accepted the laws of the land. Like morality, it is intuitive in origin and sustains and is sustained by human attributes. In its outward manifestations the hand of the artificer may be required but when a style itself is sensed as artificial it is on the downward road and its visible prostitution, whether for commercial or other motives, spells its death. The rejection of Wilson with his Downing Street pop guests and negro singers showed that at least some intuitions were not entirely blunted. For while the great mass of city and rural middle and working class have still a liking for trivial and rather vulgar entertainment, for their images of comportment they prefer conservative and patriotic styles. Britain's changed status in the world has changed none of this.

In style as in other matters one does not pick on a vague generalized 'society', blaming it for our frustrations and praising it for our satisfactions. Some individuals have a stronger sense of the fitting than others. The unknown factor is the effect on the human mind of

increasing leisure being filled in by an increasing quantity of commercialized forms of indulgence. Instinctive releases of bawdiness are one
thing and the upsurge of the bawdy in song and story in eighteenth-
century Scotland coincided with Edinburgh's intellectual Golden
Age, until both perished under the weight of English conformism. But
an unending stream of mass-produced pornography offering a vague
titillation against boredom is another thing. The propagation of
debased forms has other consequences, just as it is inspired by other
motives, than the self-found reliefs of natural coarseness. 'Oh! But I
don't see anything wrong with jazz', when spoken by an adult, tells
one a good deal about the sort of company where he or she feels most
at home. It does not matter much when one is young and animal:
youth's protection is its very animality.

'Oh! But it was worse than that in Hogarth's day', comes the
other justification, the speaker presumably identifying himself with the
prints of eighteenth-century elegance rather than with the denizens of
Gin Lane. There is however a difference between an age of naïve
relationships and one of inversion. It is the difference between animality
and morbidity. Shakespeare's rhetoric was appreciated by his contemporaries for the emotional impact of the panache of the words and not
for the introspective evocation which holds us to-day. Men who found
excitement in bear-baiting and in public mutilations and executions
reacted differently to the horror scenes of Elizabethan and Jacobean
drama: King James too had seen and encouraged murder. The more
meritorious achievements of a society are not explained, justified, nor
perpetuated by the existence of a lowest common denominator: and
in any historical movement the factors which determine it can themselves be cumulative.

The failure to recognize the nature of our problem arises para-
doxically enough from the fear of being thought old-fashioned, of
not wishing to accept innovation, in fact from a frozen orthodoxy of
revolt. The middle-aged are the worst offenders and since their illusions
of revolt were shattered by the realities of Stalinism, Resistance, and
Liberation, they can only find a romantic nostalgia in the low. The
outcome is something which in the thirties even mass unemployment
and economic distress could not accomplish—the advocacy of the
proletarian tone. Those desperately trying to move with the times
praise the man-made commercialized contrivances as the new mass-
culture: but what they are wittingly or unwittingly trying to promote
is a mass without any culture.

Yet it is no use, we have learned this before, trying to impose taste or style. The latter must first be created by and for the style setters themselves, those whom society at large envies or tries to emulate. The traditional élites have here little part to play and the particular type of emulation they inspired was only suited to naïve days when lusty people preferred lusty monarchs. Nell Gwynn could cry from her coach to the mob: 'Good people! I am the Protestant whore.' Kings would have disappointed their subjects had it been otherwise. Now the monarchy, caught up in the general process of coarsening, seems to be at the service of any commercial impresario with goods to sell or a film to show. Some other symbolic embodiment of inner need seems to be required.

'The aristocratic principle' also requires considerable qualification. From the era of the *douceur de mœurs* onwards—which is all that really concerns us—the nobility may have set fashions in clothes but was boorish enough when seen at close quarters with their perruques off, or relieving themselves in a corner of Versailles. While the Regency bucks were primping up and down St. James's, the habits which were to determine British social standards in its era of imperial supremacy were being set in more modest circles. For all the talk about Edwardian tone, the decencies which supported British life during the period of inter-war stresses and strains were not those of the well-off but of a somewhat hard-pressed professional class and of a minor gentry which was so minor that it could hardly be called a gentry.

In raffish circles aristocracy admittedly set a sort of raffish style. When Lord Lonsdale drove through Carlisle streets in the twenties, the pavements were filled with foxy-faced men in check caps, with waxed moustaches, horsy clothes, and brown leggings, cheering as 'Lordy' with side whiskers and long cigar passed by in his yellow Daimler, horn sounding like a German post coach—a style he had borrowed from the German Kaiser. Who is now the idol of Carlisle crowds, I do not know, but they look unbelievably drab and characterless. The peerage from the northern side of the Border seemed to figure once or twice a year in photographs in the local papers, either on the moors or rather pop-eyed at hunt balls. They are doubtless the models for to-day's stockbroker dream of living in Barsetshire with horse and Jaguar, and some glossy magazines strewn carefully in the lounge. A harmless illusion but a barren style, irrelevant to the lives of most of our society, and pointing to nothing.

So while there seems to be a common contemporary mood, it

N

is hardly sustaining an emotional unity. Yet it is the sense each one of us has of the quality of our fellows which will decide whether we sink deeper into inversion, indulge in mood, or move forward re-creating our contemporary experiences in forms transmissible in the future. Otherwise the Ariadne's thread of our civilization is broken. Temporal rationality does require a considerable mental effort for with its continual reassessments in time it is inherently sacrilegious, always throwing down old gods and trying to replace them by new. And the task of setting up new divinities can be undertaken neither by a multitude of bitter little internal images indulging in minor outward beatnikery, nor by the sloppy universalism which denies that there is any qualitative difference between the Trobiand Islanders and ourselves, and treats our music as merely the techniques of drawing horse-hair over cat-gut, ignoring the cultural growth behind Mozart, Beethoven, or Schubert. When the price we are asked to pay is the pollution of our sensitivity to finer things, it is time to ring down the curtain.

For Caliban wants desperately to rise up, be identified as a man, and give his loyalty to those who recognize him as one. The crime against him is that it pays to keep him down as a monster. Only a sense of discrimination, for one thing as being finer than another, can release him from bondage, and give him identity. Our cultural creations are not autonomous like flint axes, scientific applications, or functional institutions. Artistic creation and re-creation remain linked to us since they originate from our experience and not from the objects alone. Metaphor is our intuition and suffers from our degradation.

The artist, presumably in an even more heightened state of self-consciousness than the rest of us, is caught up in the centre of this conflict. On him falls the main burden of contributing to the style of the time and reproducing it in communicable forms. The traditional disciplines through which he can express himself have become doubly repellent by their subjection to non-human, or at least non-intuitive, forces. If he senses the predicament of men trapped by self-created images which no longer satisfy, he will turn away even more violently from representational techniques. Fighting back against this, Francis Bacon succeeds in representing the tortured relationship between outer and inner man, the frustrated apes in their vaguely human trappings, and the sacrificial version of Man which turns out to be butcher meat. If for Michelangelo the flesh reflected the soul it imprisoned, Bacon brings out both our disgust at the outer flesh and our inward terror.

Within each generation we can identify more or less where we hit a barrier. The protests of other generations from which we are emotionally detached seem aimless to non-participants and consequently develop the appearance of a sad sort of orthodoxy. But now the objects of protest, some ill-defined and resented ascendancy, are so vaguely identifiable that they seem to dissolve as soon as the protest has begun to pay off as a West End success. But still no general style with communicable relationships of words, forms, and musical notes shows signs of emerging. Better no images at all, or at best allusive ones which will fit in with everybody's moods of doubt and *Angst!* The technique for this, not being difficult to master, degenerates into 'pop art' or just plain phoneyness and we spot too easily that it has become triviality and is indistinguishable from the ad-mass decorative associations from which in practice it derives much of its origins. And if the truly sensitive artist cannot find the liberating metaphor to produce new transitions between objects of consciousness, he will only proclaim the message that all human experience is incoherence and purpose is an illusion. So we have metaplasm instead of metaphor, happenings instead of creation, and shirts thrown at the canvas.

Where artistic experience has become a self-conscious chase after immediacy and spontaneity, regression of this sort is a natural outcome. Infantilism, primitivism, orgiastic forms of self-expression, and the cult of the negro offer outlets with the excuse of some non-æsthetic commitment, so that cultural activity becomes entangled in the same universal pseudo-moralities under cloak of which political scapegoat hunting is conducted. In this situation the artist has even to falsify his experience to himself. If the negroes he depicts are not to lend ammunition to our intuitive reactions against an alien identity, they must not be made too spontaneous or immediate. But if they are presented as virtuous like white bourgeois, they fail as symbols of spontaneity. So the cult becomes a dishonest titillation like the Crime-Does-Not-Pay films with special pleading to make allowances for everything. And a sad aspect of the proclaimed universal quality of our culture, apart from the deleterious effect it has on our own capacity for discrimination, is that other peoples of the contemporary world who are uncertain of their identity, such as Turks or Latin Americans, set about composing in our contemporary fashion as if their own figurative and decorative traditions had never existed.

If we look back through the history of European styles, innovation was less novel than it seemed to contemporaries. It was basically a restatement and since the main *Kulturträger* of the European tradition were such compelling intuitive creators, and their metaphors so powerful, in every new 'contemporary occasion' the emotional unity of their creations can be relived. Artists have often caught up the most unlikely moods and re-created their experience as things of beauty. But if we are conscious anarchists for too long, the cultural break may be too complete to be rejoined. Anarchists are by definition unable to communicate about any subject except anarchism and in an era of inversion there could be a nasty convergence when the emotional intensity associated with æsthetic frustration coincides with self-justification.

So the recovery of style means gathering up our intuitive links with Europe's cultural past just as in the political field we have to rejoin the European process of creating new institutions. If the artistic creations which inspire our imagination are dispersed as general chattels, we expose ourselves to the same hobgoblins which haunt us in ethics and politics. Our need to share human insights is doubly clamant since one of men's oldest intuitive relationships, that with their gods, is being rapidly destroyed by those whose task it is to serve them. For the need to revere remains and perhaps a profound sense of melancholy, such as Burckhardt described as spreading through the late classical world, underlies the *comoedia diabolica* which we currently accept as the human lot. 'The example of Christ', which we are inter-mittently urged to follow, eludes us the moment we try to find the historical Christ who, if he ever existed, is for ever lost under a mass of contradictory writings. Christian can in practice never be anything else than Christian does, *und wie es christelt wird so judelt sich auch.*

So the priests either try to restore their authority by playing on their flocks' sense of insecurity or guilt, or like the hippy Anglican bishops desecrate their cathedrals with sex shows, Maori dances, and the like. We have had all this before with counter-productive results, so why do they persist? In the twenties, Scottish township life was frequently invaded by young and idealistic ministers who introduced church services with light music and magic-lantern slides. It still made no difference to the numbers of the faithful so that to-day the centre of the Covenanting faith, the presbyteries of the Border country, bear witness to dwindling flocks and closed churches. Those who wanted to hear light music and look at slides came and departed as do those who now attend progressive communion services with beat and sex: the gods die because there is no one to bring them votive offerings.

But if Western Christianity has lost its claim to universality, it can still demonstrate its place in the continuity of our civilization. The past intuitions of a religion which began by denying the flesh are most intensely communicated to us to-day through the artist's representations of human emotions. Our present-day objects of reverence, our embodiments of compassion, are the creations of secular artists of the Middle Ages and the Renaissance and link us to similar creations of the classical world. As the crude instinctive elements of religion receded in our minds, our emotions suffused their own enjoyment over the creations so that the representations speak to us of the god's humanity where the priest and theologian can tell us nothing. All the arts have participated with us in this process and from Giotto onwards through Michelangelo, Rembrandt, Shakespeare, Beethoven and Wagner we feel linked to a universal truth.

There is certainly no risk to society if monolithic notions of divinity go into discard along with those of Man. Whatever the Church of England may be now it is not the Tory Party at prayer. Where priests have lost their vocation or where, as in America, faith has become attached to inessentials rather than to articles and has become a community status badge, society loses no restraint.[7] A society will be 'moral' when its rulers encourage the *mores* which sustain family life and increase the people's sense of security so that their human qualities can develop. It is not the task of government to impose the 'Golden Rule' nor indeed to impose its own or anyone else's notion of the fitting. But it is its task to ensure that the law allows those who are offended or distressed by the conduct of others to obtain ready redress.

If the Tories are to live up to their promise to introduce a new style into government and encourage individual responsibility, they must be seen once and for all to be rejecting the argument that, because people obey the laws, the individual must have his choices determined for him by law. The totality of measures of the last decades decreeing how a subject must dispose of his own property, what must be his choices in education, work, and companions, making crimes of the

---

[7] 'God likes regular people—people who play baseball like movie nuns. He smiles on society and his message is a relaxing one. He does not scold you: he does not demand of you. He is a gregarious God and he can be found in the smiling happy people of the society about you. As the advertisements put it, religion can be fun.' W. H. Whyte, *The Organization Man* (Allen Lane: The Penguin Press), Chapter 20. So we finish up logically with 'Jesus-Superstar' and 'Jesus-Freaks'.

normal preferences of English and Scots for each other, ordering the individual to participate in this or denying him participation in the other, have meant that the law, instead of protecting him, has become arbitrary. The closed corporations of the legal profession make a mockery of the ordinary subject's right to justice, the state penalizes the innocent by refusing to pay the costs of even the actions it loses, only the very brave and very rich may challenge arbitrariness and while in matters of decency some are given the right to offend, the majority is denied the right to challenge offence. An out-of-date system of courts clogged up with antique procedures stands in the way of speedy and fair hearings.

So a massive programme of reform of what was after all the first and central role of government is an essential part of the restoration of faith in our institutions, a scrapping of repressive and discriminatory laws, the reorganization of courts and procedures to permit the individual to bring his complaints and make his case without cost if need be. A vast sweeping away of the byzantine rackets of the legal profession and the hocus-pocus of courts will make the subjects feel that the law is theirs and is an ordering principle. The risks of our becoming a litigious society are preferable to those of our becoming a criminal one. When we know that the laws will help us to defend our shared inheritance of custom, our *mores* will be in less danger than they are at present.

But this inheritance can only be shared by those whose identity is linked to the objectivity of institutions. This requires not only the removal of the latter-day version of the Saracen camps, the non-European communities which through error were allowed to settle in our cities, but also that Britain in turn should be prepared to share in the new growth of European institutions. With the other countries of the Western European seaboard, Britain forms a continuum of thought and culture: we shall inevitably be affected by their movements of ideas, by their ordering concepts, as well as by their economic and military policies. Our own society will certainly feel the impact of the doubtful loyalties of France and Italy, the emotional conflicts of the German mind, and material calculations of Belgians and Dutch. But to remain passive means accepting the consequences without being able to direct events: to participate means joining in the process of reshaping Europe and determining our own identity. The European society which will emerge, however slowly and painfully, will bring about new transitions, disrupt closed corporations, break up monopolies and cliques, and result in a new vocabulary of daily usage. It will be a society where we shall have to act transitively, in the sense of operating beyond ourselves. But this is the traditional European process which creates bastions to identity and can command loyalties.

Is there another course? As Asia and Africa determine their actions in terms of their own advantage, so must we. Our concepts of political purpose cannot be stretched to appease non-Europeans: their subject-centred societies permit of no objective institutions. We can only leave them with their sense of the particular and their instinct for juxtaposition while we consider what new definitions are required within the Western world, notably between Europe and America. 'We are in great haste to construct a magnetic telegraph from Maine to Texas', wrote Thoreau. 'But Maine and Texas, it may be, have nothing important to communicate.' There is a yawning spiritual gap which will never be closed by heartier back-slapping, ever more potent dry martinis, or the establishment of a PX on the moon. The Americans will find their own answer. They have thinkers who, like Machiavelli and Clausewitz, dare to think about the unthinkable, and the impact of their thoughts on Europe will be incommensurable. But we do not have to follow the Americans through their process.

Persistence in our present course points only to impossible attempts to combine incompatibles, to evasions of reality, and to betrayal rather than the admission of error; and finally to violence which will not be revolutionary but criminal, aimless, and neurotic in its nature, bringing counter-action with unforeseeable local conflict until harsh authority is reimposed. Abyssinia remains as a warning of what happens when a political system has outlived its day. The Turks, last of the purely instinctive conquerors who built up their empire with little more than swords and horses, have been left with deep emotions, a resentful dependence on American strategists, and W.C.s which fail to flush. When the Iranians gave up the military effort to impose a new order on the Middle East in place of the hierarchical systems based on fear, placation of death, and on sacrifice, they had hardly grasped the dimension of time but had managed to reconcile surface contradictions sufficiently to humanize the Jews, create a cosmic imagery which Christianity later took over, and, as older memories of empire faded under Arab, Turki, and Tartar invasions, retain a sense of the underlying incongruity of things. So they could still laugh and, while professing the teachings of the Prophet, enjoy their very potable wines until the day came when they were wooed for their oil. Doubtless in a shabby back-water of half-caste communalism and inured to the sound of sporadic small-arms fire in their city streets, the British will nourish both resentment and consolation.

It may not happen. It need never happen. A framework of laws which binds rulers and offers subjects redress against arbitrariness and grievance will revive the sense of a king's peace. A future monarch could add his personal style to legitimacy and from the new sense of fitting can come a new sense of community. It may be a community where we invoke authority more than we do freedom—for just as the lyric demands the highest poetic discipline, so too new emotional demands require the compensation of a heightened sense of style. This represents no risk to our liberties as we have created them in Europe. Since inner need rather than outer necessity has been the determinant, there has been something of the artist's approach in all great European endeavours and the arts themselves have never been an autonomous sector of society. It is in the transitions of life that the need for form is felt most strongly, form which confers its authority on statuary, form which gives painting its gravity and calm, and endows architecture with its proportion and music with its power. When this is a live need in society, the artist's own desire for participation will gather up old symbols, metaphors, and forms and transmute them into new creations. And if we have retained our sense of common heritage, these creations will also win our allegiance.

And freedom in Europe is not a static condition but freedom to face the risks of action. Curiosity has been the mother of European invention and created a pace and rhythm different from those of non-European peoples, so that our quality of enjoyment is linked not to indulgence and contentment but to the restlessness of individual assertion. In a transitive society this assertion can find its satisfaction in conscious individual purpose and in new purposeful communal applications of our historical privileges. The counter to treason is for life itself to offer self-knowledge through action instead of retreat to fantasy inner worlds where treachery and loyalty are all one.

Over a century and a half of British history, the Conservative Party has found that once in office it can look to a decade or more of power if its leaders prove themselves as administrators. They have now to be something more. Opportunity is given them to create the institutions within which human attributes can be the stabilizing factors in change, when one man in his life can play many parts and serve his fellow-lieges with human loyalties.

Index

Index